K

PASSIONATE SOCIOLOGY

PASSIONATE SOCIOLOGY

Ann Game and
Andrew Metcalfe

SAGE Publications
London • Thousand Oaks • New Delhi

Extract from *Madeline* by Ludwig Bemelmans. Copyright
1939 by Ludwig Bemelmans, renewed © 1967 by
Madeleine Bemelmans and Barbara Bemelmans Marciano.
Used by permission of Viking Penguin, a division of
Penguin Books USA Inc.

First published 1996

SAGE Publications Ltd
6 Bonhill Street
London EC2A 4PU

SAGE Publications Inc
2455 Teller Road
Thousand Oaks, California 91320

SAGE Publications India Pvt Ltd
32, M-Block Market
Greater Kailash – I
New Delhi 110 048

British Library Cataloguing in Publication data

A catalogue record for this book is available
from the British Library

ISBN 0 8039 7460-4
ISBN 0 8039 7461 2 (pbk)

Library of Congress catalog record available

Typeset by M Rules
Printed in Great Britain by Redwood Books,
Trowbridge, Wiltshire

Contents

Acknowledgements

Dedicated to the joy, and pain, of university teaching, this book sets out what we have learned from teaching sociology together for five years. It's a celebration of the rich rewards of collegiality, of the books and writers we love, of a passionate sociology's capacity to quicken our appreciation and pleasure in the art of life, of the students who have been our teachers.

One of the joys of university life is its potential for excessive generosity. Academic life can be a feast to which everyone contributes, whether or not they mean to, whether or not their gifts are used as they intended. Such a feast produces a magical economy where strict reciprocity is impossible and scarcity loses its threat, where teachers and students always get more back than they've given and sometimes more than they've bargained for.

We can therefore name only a few of those who've contributed to this book. Sal Renshaw commented on both our first and second drafts and we've benefited immeasurably from her detailed suggestions and her generous encouragement. Gay Hawkins, Annette Kuhn, Ian Lennie, Maddie Oliver and Anita Sibrits also made valuable suggestions on our drafts. Seminar audiences in Sydney, Adelaide and Lancaster commented on various working papers; we learned much about metaphor from a subject we taught with Jenny Lloyd; Leo and Max Sibrits have made a deep impact on several chapters; John Bern conducted the interview discussed in *Ink*. The editors of *Work, Employment & Society* have permitted republication of a few paragraphs from Andrew Metcalfe's article 'The Curriculum Vitae' (1992: 619–41), and Scholastic kindly allowed us to quote Ludwig Bemelmans' *Madeline*.

Our colleagues Michael Humphrey, Diana Olsberg and Gay Hawkins, and our Head of School Ann Daniel and Dean John Ingleson have our gratitude for creating a school environment where teaching and learning can be joyous and open.

As a way of appropriately acknowledging all the other people who've contributed to the feast that sustains us, we've done our best to write a generous book. There's a traditional storytellers' ending that appeals to us –

Take it, and may the next one who tells it better it.

Passion

[to] arrive at an ever more precise and at the same time ever more passionate apprehension of the tangible world. (Breton, quoted in Nadeau 1973: 37)

The combination of passion and sociology can have an unsettling, almost vertiginous effect. Many professional sociologists have described the combination as a contradiction in terms, the immediate response to our title being one of shock or laughter – 'you can't do that'. By asking questions about sociology and its relation to passion, we aim to destabilise forms of sociology that regard this juxtaposition as inappropriate. More importantly, we want to advocate and demonstrate a sociology that is intrigued and driven by this type of juxtaposition.

The term 'sociology' stands splendidly alone in many textbook and journal titles, as if its meaning came not from circuits of language but from a direct correspondence to a fixed entity in the real world, as if the word simply *named* a discipline. When textbook sociology encounters students unsure of its nature, it confidently distributes a definition, something bland like 'the science of society'. When it pairs 'sociology' with familiar adjectives, like 'empirical', 'critical', 'classical', it acts as if the joint meaning of the adjective and its noun were a simple combination of two independent terms. The identity, sociology, remains.

But when 'sociology' is joined to passion, a word from a foreign domain of meaning, the discipline is disconcerted. Readers are jolted from conventional into metaphoric ways of thinking, allowing new meanings to be imagined. Besides disturbing the fantasy of sociology as a discrete identity, the shock highlights the metaphoric principle at work in all meaning processes. Rather than being directly present in words, meaning, including the meaning of sociology, is generated through shifting relations *between* words or signs. Sociology is constituted in social relations like those it studies.

This book is as much concerned with this process of combination, with the creativity of metaphor, as it is with the specific combination – passion and sociology. Passionate sociology has many kinds of reverberation for us, and our appreciation of its meanings is still emerging. We value this process, and rather than wishing to define passionate sociology, we hope it will set off reverberations for others too – that meanings will continue to emerge.

* * *

I love reading tales of passion, of love and death, joy and pain, of fate. At the same time I dread these stories and the awful bruised feeling that will inevitably overwhelm me as I read. By story's end, my hands will tremble as I turn the pages. What sort of awe is this? It is more than the fear that strong emotions inconveniently diminish our control over our lives. Passion is savage because the extremes to which it takes us are inevitably the limits of our existence. With its assurance of pain and death, passion reminds us of our corporeality, of the primitive truths of bodily finitude that many would rather forget. These are losses that biology, medicine, psychology and sociology cannot remedy, for all their pomp and therapeutic promises.

The word 'passion' loses some of its profound resonances when taken to mean no more than strong emotion, usually involving love or sexual desire. Nevertheless, its corporeal and spiritual implications linger, even within this usage. Passion's first definition in the *Oxford English Dictionary* is 'the suffering of pain', a general sense reverberating with the particular sufferings of Christ and other martyrs. Diseases and disorders of the body also come under this heading. The second definition concerns 'the fact or condition of being acted upon or affected by external agency', passion being related here to passivity. It is only in the third general meaning, 'an affection of the mind', that passion begins to resemble its modern debased usage, the definition referring to vehement feelings, overpowering emotions, outbursts of temper, amorous feelings and sexual desire. These sets of meanings are more connected than they initially appear, the third set implying the first and second. Passion's insistence on pain and fate is so awesome that many of us shelter in its reduced usage.

What gives passion its power is its veiled association with death. When I hold a loved one passionately, it is the intimation of mortality that gives the experience its edge, sharpness and depth. Every touch has the comfort and desolation of the first experiences of oneness and separation. At the same time, each touch may be the last one. The child I hold so tenderly will inevitably leave me, and is leaving me every day, as he grows. His changes delight me, but each has the sting of loss. I might respond by trying to love him to death, devouring him with my camera in an attempt to capture him as he is, so that he cannot be taken from me. In willing myself to look more sharply, smell more deeply, touch more sensitively, hear more profoundly, I push my body to its sensual limits, to reach and reach beyond the limits of his corporeal form. But I'm doomed to fail, not only because I can never capture enough, but because I will inevitably forget. His growth also brings the ache of knowing that I will probably leave him, perhaps when he's least prepared for it. For his life, so dear to me, implies my death. These are experiences of passion from which I can protect neither of us.

One of the dictionary's final definitions of passion is 'an eager outreaching of the mind towards something'. In a sense, this 'something' is always our bodily limits. The edge on which I tremble in passion is always death, the sharpness always pain, the depth always the substance of my corporeal form. It's not that the body's finitude *intrudes* on the experience of desire, or that I would wish it away; as I only know what I experience through my mortal body, this *constitutes* my passion. Passion is the form of mortal desire. The relation that rends my heart is the source of my joy. It is death's whisper that gives my life its scale and meaning, that tells me I'm alive. Passion is *extreme* not because of the extent or strength of our emotions, but because it deals with unreasonable, unmanageable and final things. It is foreign because it inevitably confronts the mysteries of birth and death. The strange tears that well up when I look at my perfect sleeping child are tears not of love alone, but of love and loss together.

Passion's association with life's limits can make it a rude and frightening force, especially in a century that has often prided itself on its technological and economic victory over finitude. Just as death is medicalised and quarantined in western society, grand passion has come to seem an old-fashioned idea. The implications of its power are repressed in the same way that civilisation is said to have tamed nature, the body, the primitive and the irrational – the realms where passion supposedly resides. Modern sciences like psychology and sociology rarely talk about passions, and certainly not their own. The closest they come is through the more anaemic concept of emotions. For most psychologists and sociologists, the idea of passion is as imprecise and pre-scientific as humoral understandings of health.

Yet our culture is not passionless, even if the dominant expressions are of a passion conveniently trimmed of grandeur and unreasonableness. Passion's darker, wilder forms still prowl unacknowledged around the outskirts of our rationality. Were they really banished or domesticated, we wouldn't constantly need to reassure ourselves of our control over them. We cushion ourselves because secretly we remain in awe of them. While we tell ourselves that we fear some primal force from our past, in our hearts we recognise this force as our present mortal condition.

* * *

What, then, of passionate sociology? Fear of mortality is vividly displayed in common forms of academic knowledge, including the more traditional sociologies that present knowledge as something dispassionate and disembodied, a product of the mind rather than the heart, body or soul. Such knowledges desire to rise above the partiality of the knower's embodied form, preferring to experience the world as a set of fixed and external objects. Bodies have particular limited qualities, particular places in the world, particular life spans; objective knowledge, however, has no specific qualities or location and can pronounce eternal truths. It offers a cure for the finitude of the flesh, but its abstraction comes at the cost of a loss of edge, sharpness and depth. The loss is evident in the recent revival of sociological interest in embodiment and emotion, which mostly treats 'the body' and 'the emotions' as objects, and objects uninvolved in the studies themselves. Scores of disembodied and dispassionate studies paradoxically urge the significance of bodies and emotions.

If traditional sociology has masterfully refused to place itself within the social life it studies, our book's title suggests a commitment to such reflexivity. By attending closely to the social processes involved in the generation of sociological knowledge, we refigure conventional distinctions between poetry and practicality and between theory, method and ethics. We want to demystify the abstraction of most sociological theory and open it to students' own creative practices. Our title also flags our sociological interest in the passions and corporeality of sociality, alluding to the importance of recognising desire within sociology. The desire to know is itself one of the most powerful passions, motivated by desires to know one's own self. The structure of these desires changes the forms of knowledge produced and privileged.

In attempting to master death, traditional sociology denies life. Passionate sociology's practices, on the contrary, are not based on otherworldly aspirations to the Eternal or Absolute, and thus can recognise that they are part of life. Passionate sociology celebrates an immersion in life, a compassionate involvement with the world and with others. It is a sociology concerned with the sharp and specific experiences of life; not seeking to dissolve these experiences in the pursuit of idealised abstraction, it wants to *feel* them, to be on the edge. An engaged or passionate sociology involves a sensual and full-bodied approach to knowing and to practices of knowledge such as reading, writing, teaching; it is risk-taking; and it allows for an open, playful and mutual relation between writers and readers, and teachers and students. Although sociology has traditionally denied the dependence of writers on readers and teachers on students, we recognise that passion, social life and sociology only exist in the in-between, in specific and moving social *relations*.

Passionate sociology promises to enrich life, in the manner of metaphor, by expanding the possibilities and choices sociality offers. By practising a passionate sociology in this book, offering a passionate sociological account of sociology, we hope to inspire readers to participate in creative processes that sharpen and deepen experience, and move the meanings of passionate sociology beyond our present imaginings.

School

Knowledge doesn't spring fully formed from genius or revelation. Nor does it exist abstractly, in 'thought', before being expressed in one or another form. Right from the start, knowledge is produced through intimate and tempestuous relationships with these organised forms, which are the constraints necessary for cultural production. The point was appreciated by Isadora Duncan: if she could say what a dance meant, she said, she wouldn't need to dance. Boris Pasternak understood it too: despite fearing repression in the USSR, he feared exile more, for the institutional forms of Russian and Soviet society were the preconditions of his work. And in this book we argue that sociological thinking–writing is an organisation of forms, of institutions, words, metaphors, stories, concepts, topics, themes. Even if writing begins with an intuition, it isn't the presentation or unfolding of a pre-existing piece of truth, for the 'piece' is patch-work and the showing of it a piece of theatre. If organisation limits sociological writing and reading, it is also its precondition.

We are interested, then, in the cultural forms and practices that generate sociological knowledge, and we will begin in this chapter with the institutions of the academy, which are the setting and mediation of our reading and writing. While many non-academics romanticise universities as institutions that protect free thought from external interference, many academics grumble that they're places where thought is obstructed by the insatiable demands of students and bureaucrats. Both views imply that universities should be institutionally hollow, ivy-covered walls safeguarding the free movement of untamed thought within. We prefer the view that universities are a social and technical organisation of cultural labour. Rather than being hollow, they are the complex form in relation to which a type of thought is shaped.

Academic thought generates physics, medicine and nuclear bombs, it produces doctors, lawyers, architects and sociologists, it remakes our self-understandings, and it is the basis of this book, even when we criticise its metaphysical pretensions. But for all its power and excitement, academic thought remains one form of knowledge among others, neither transparent nor absolute. It is a specific institutional product.

One aim of this chapter is to show how the institutions of universities and academic disciplines shape sociology and its practitioners; another is to reflect on the student–teacher relation. The chapter was originally called *Scandal*, because the institutionality of school life is a scandal to the fantasy of pure knowledge, but we've swapped *School* for *Scandal* to clarify our purpose. Our aim is neither to debunk university disciplines for their failure to fulfil a fantasy, nor to defend all the existing organisational arrangements within sociology. As sociologists working in a university, we're not posing the utopia of a non-institutional knowledge; we're instead insisting that there are ways to unsettle the terrible demand for pure and absolute knowledge and ways to imagine and conduct different sociological relations. Sociology must be ordered, but it could have a different order.

* * *

My parents sent me to a primary school fancy dress parade as the Absent-Minded Professor who'd forgotten his trousers. I wasn't sure what a professor was, but I sensed a respect that tempered my trouserless embarrassment, especially when the costume won a prize. Decades later I found that absent-minded academics really do fuss and flap around university corridors, wearing their disorganisation as proud proof of the Higher Things on their minds. Such academics leave faculty and university administration to 'intellectual has-beens' and 'careerists' whom they scornfully position outside the production of knowledge. Urgent requests for simple timetable information sink forever in their clutter. 'Oh, they're hopeless at organisation,' postgraduates laugh indulgently, 'it's concepts we get from them' – as if concepts weren't forms of intellectual organisation.

Ironically, these presentations of the disorganised academic self are organised, around a denial of organisation. The institution giving academics their tenure and offices and lecterns and libraries and computers and classes and study leave and community respect and wages is ordered as the profane that academics shun to affirm their sacred and purely intellectual calling. The dirt of a High-Minded Academic is the clean of an efficient and managed workplace, their pure the dirt of a cluttered desk (see Douglas 1970).

The honour of dirt is a common religious practice, signifying that one's spiritual home is beyond this world. In the academic case, however, this practice is rarely accompanied by a rejection of the worldly benefits of universities. Heaven help the Head of School who limits the academics' access to the business cards and international phone calls whose cost is too trivial to concern intellectuals. Woe betide the school secretary if the photocopy paper isn't ordered. For many academics who complain about the *organisation* of universities, nothing could be worse than being outside these institutions. Outside they really *would* be naked, with no one looking on in amused respect.

Academic production is characterised by its daily dependence on the discipline, organisation, management and power that constitute universities. This book, for example, arises from our own difficult relation with the academy, a relation sharing some of the passion and frustration of Duncan's dependence on dance and Pasternak's on Russia. The academy gives us the opportunity to write, the forms in which to write, the bodies of literature to address, a position to write from, an audience to write to, a market for our publishers – and in doing so it provides the frustrating constraints that fuel our desire to write and write differently. We claim to offer a contribution to sociological knowledge because we use concepts and arguments and forms used in other works generally accepted as sociological. Perhaps more important, however, this book is sociological because we can demonstrate our integration into a disciplinary community organised around academic journals, conferences, friendships, professional associations and, especially, university departments.

When establishing these departments, universities don't simply acknowledge pre-existing entities. Sociology has no natural boundaries and without its university location it would be an even more diffuse set of amateur interests found in irregular journals, societies and conferences. The first sociology schools in universities licensed certain people to organise sociology by ranking these diffuse interests. The founders used the universities' status and legal standing to produce themselves as sociologists, their writings as sociological and their students as sociologists. Subsequently each new department, each academic appointment and each graduate redefines the discipline. Sociology's history is not, therefore, a history of ideas but an intellectual–institutional history, a matter of blackboards and budgets.

Because of their specific characteristics as workplaces, modern universities generate new forms of knowledge production. Accordingly academic sociology has refined and intensified its disciplinary practices, so that more people work under greater surveillance on often narrower issues. Sociological qualifications, types of research, areas of research, ways of publishing and rates of publication are monitored and managed by university appointment, promotion and research committees, by journal editors and by research funding bodies. Through its university location, sociological research is also bound closely to teaching. Obviously, teaching produces the next generation of researchers, most of whom begin producing research while still (postgraduate) students. But other bonds also connect teaching to research. Books like this exist because of student markets; libraries can support scores of specialised sociology journals because they also provide student services; research areas tend to be identified through the curriculum divisions used in job advertisements; curriculum and subject design requires lecturers to mark out and ritually affirm their understandings of sociology's nature. In all these ways, academic modes of knowledge production create particular forms of knowledge.

Universities also produce apparently enclosed knowledges, despite operating across national boundaries. Sociology appears *contained* in its journals, monographs, lectures, textbooks and university departments; university libraries and academics are treated as repositories of knowledge, and students attend not to produce knowledge but to drink from its cup. This containment is a fantasy, but academics are still expected to be masters of their field, capable of 'magisterial' judgements. To attain this status, PhD students are conventionally required to produce a

comprehensive literature review as the first step to demonstrating their own 'significant and original contribution to the sum
total of knowledge'. The value of individual contributions to
academic knowledge relies on the fancy that, somewhere, there
is a sum total.

These disciplinary and academic contexts are the forms in
which we live, with which we struggle; they are our necessary
limitations. If not especially romantic, they only seem tawdry
beside the clean fantasies of intellectuals who see and record truth
directly, in all its brilliance. Acknowledgement of this dependence on organisation cannot lead to the elimination of
institutionality, but it may change the forms of knowledge produced.

* * *

The students most likely to attend university have turned school
disciplines into self-disciplines, aligning particular ways of thinking with particular deportments. If I arrive late at a class's first
tutorial, I usually find that students have left vacant the chair
closest to the blackboard. Through habit, they've turned themselves into a class and me into a schoolteacher whose authority
and knowledge are signified by control over the sacred chalk.
The smell of chalk dust magically turns adults into schoolchildren
who react to deeply embodied commands: 'have your pens and
paper ready', 'face the front', 'be quiet when the teacher is speaking', 'write down what's on the board'.

The first sociology assignment we set seeks to highlight the
assumptions institutionalised within university education by
asking students to observe one of their classes and analyse its
micro-rituals and power relations. Consider the pedagogic relations built into a lecture theatre. The tendency for the stepped
seating to direct students' eyes to the lecturer is reinforced by the
fixed rows, which make it hard for students to see their neighbours, much less all their colleagues. Students are thus
segregated, depersonalised, quantified, as one among many,
potentially in competition, and they are pinned in this confined
position by the writing desks that fold down in front of them.
Lecturers, on the other hand, may be able to see all students, so
that ideally one objectifying look can silence any murmuring

student. This places lecturers in a God-like position, and an impression of omniscience is fortified by the lectern, which turns their script into scripture; by the lighting that sanctifies them and leaves students in the half-light; by the placement of the clock, which allows them to monitor time beyond the vision of students; by their power over the microphone and brilliance of the overhead projector, technologies for making their words larger than life; by the imbalance between their talk and the students' silence, their presentations of personality and the students' anonymous mass; by their demiurgic capacity to make things happen, to move at will, while everyone else is reduced to stasis. Lecturers are a fullness and students a blank page to be filled. Of course, power relations actually ebb and flow, with students able to subvert lecturers' power and override the architectural codes, but the codes must still be overcome. Students and lecturers renegotiate their positions from the confined positions in which architects put them.

In its obsession with separating teachers from students, the lecture theatre encodes a common academic desire to protect pure research vocations from the 'distraction' and potential 'contamination' of teaching. Because this separation is threatened by the messy intimacy of tutorials, these usually have less status than lectures and a greater capacity to induce panic in academics. Such fears and barriers exist because intellectual privilege is threatened by acknowledgement of the academic's close dependence on students. The teacher–student relation matches the colonial relation between civilised and primitive, students positioned as the nightmare of intellectual insecurity on whom academics rely to distinguish their own dream of intellectual security. But defined this way, students become a threat against whom academics must erect barriers: because students resemble academics in many ways, their proximity highlights the academics' own insecurity. The biggest fear is that academics may learn something from teaching, for if students produce doubts in the academic, they unsettle the academic's intellectual mastery and challenge the common basis of academic distinction.

Students' observations and evaluations of teachers circulate in lecture hall foyers and university coffee shops, and although they rarely receive official recognition, they allow students to demystify some of the academics' claims to knowledge and privilege.

Our observation exercise invites students to develop this knowledge by bringing it from the university's margins into the sacred space of classrooms and assignments, an act of deterritorialisation that disturbs conventional understandings of teaching. By asking students and teachers to become self-conscious about the mediations of teaching, down to apparent details – lecturers clearing their throats to command silence, students choosing where to sit and what to write – this unsettling of convention offers more than 'a better understanding of teaching'. Once aware of the rituals constituting the lecture, students no longer see it as transparent communication, a matter of the lecturer's output becoming their input. By returning the lecturer's objectifying gaze, their observations change the lecture relationship, enhancing their capacity to manage the interchange. These issues are taken up in the chapters *Managing* and *Desire*.

If such an exercise changes the lecture relationship, it cannot simply deinstitutionalise university knowledge, a fact demonstrated by the grade that must be assigned to the students' observation exercises. In the terms of Foucault's *Discipline and Punish* (1977a: 170ff), grading involves surveillance, normalisation and examination. By observing and measuring students against a norm, teachers convert them to marks, homogenising them as numbers and ranks recorded in individualised files, reducing their specific qualities to quantities. Grading also suppresses the qualities of different knowledges, for in the absence of alternative criteria, a numerical mark presents itself as the measurement of some single and finite 'thing', suggesting that a 75.5 per cent essay possesses just over three-quarters of 'the answer'.

How do academics know what an essay is worth, to the 0.5 per cent? They know *because* they're academics, because it's what they're paid to do, the ability to mark serving as a proof that they embody the standards of their discipline. They are the singularity, finitude and whole against which they measure percentages. The knowledge contained in the body of the university teacher synecdochically signifies the universities' containment of bodies of knowledge. This accounts for the reluctance to give 100 per cent: as a synecdoche for the whole discipline, it is the teacher who holds full knowledge, and a distance must be kept between this position and the student.

The academic bluff of the grade cannot be sustained with post-graduate students, whose theses are finally simply accepted or rejected, with examiners' comments. Leaving space for open and plural notions of knowledge and truth, this is also the form of assessment applied to the manuscripts of academics. The abandonment of the undergraduate grade occurs partly because thesis examiners no longer dare claim to measure the 100 per cent, and partly because a graded PhD hints at the possibility of grading academics too, a suggestion that horrifies lecturers yearning for the safe place where they are whole, where everyone knows that academics simply know.

Each mark that academics dispense can temper their own fear of grades, by confirming their separation from students. As markers, their position is as secure, asocial and autonomous as truth. Allegiance to this fantasy doesn't mean that academics don't care about students, or that they don't care what students think of them, but within the objective grading process these are repressed or marginalised concerns. Academics crave the students who vindicate them by desiring their knowledge, but this can remain a safely secret dependence.

These complex cycles of recognition, identification, evaluation and denial are commemorated in university graduations. The solemn parade of academics in esoteric garb as timeless as truth itself; the last ceremonial roll call of students' names, honouring the heroes who have survived since the first roll call of primary school; the solemn awarding of the degree on its heavy paper with its self-important calligraphy and its red seal; the respectful audience of strangers, family and friends, so reminiscent of a christening, marriage or death: this is for many the apotheosis of university. Before witnesses, graduations solemnise the grading of certified knowledge and the awarding of new identity.

Graduations are often seen as high points of academic collegiality. This communion is based not on common employment in an institution that requires examinations, but on commemoration of the academics' shared capacity to measure knowledge. Whatever shame academics feel about grading is lost in the ceremony's urgent desire to honour their knowledge and assessments. Teachers look on proudly as their students graduate, but the pride is that students have vindicated them by becoming disciples, the personal warmth of teaching relations becoming a warm feeling of the teacher's own security. The students' passage in the academic footsteps is ritually enacted when they ascend from the body of the hall to the sacred podium where lectures are normally delivered and where the academics are now assembled. Through their ascent, their doffing hats, their handshake with the Chancellor and the baton-like handover of the testamur, students touch the academic condition. But the touch is momentary. The student returns to the floor of the hall. Academics touch students only to affirm their own primary relation, a direct relation to knowledge.

Students are both the precondition of the teacher's position and a threat to the academic self-image. To insist on a sacred relation to truth, academics must keep a distance from students, repressing the constant reminders that both students and teachers participate in the profane institution of the university. Recognition of this institutionality confounds the transparency model of teaching and demystifies notions of sacred academics and revealed knowledge.

* * *

Academics may be spared the open humiliation of having their work graded, but juries of peers are constantly assessing, accepting or rejecting it. Peer reviews are to the 'scholarly community' what grades are to the student–teacher relation, and some peers are decidedly more equal than others. Academics are examined every time they deliver a paper or send an article to a journal or a book manuscript to a publisher, every time they apply for a job or promotion or research grant, every time a performance appraisal is conducted. Peer reviews occur whenever one academic attends another's lecture, a practice often discouraged for this reason, and they occur throughout the production of a book like this. The scholarly community is an organisation of the disciplinary power to assess.

In any corridor there are academics frozen by their horror of this judgement. Such people cannot write for fear they will be exposed as the impostors they fear themselves to be. Their past 'successes' bring little relief if they believe they've since lost 'it', the required luck or genius. In the same corridor are academics who publish regularly but whose work has a joyless hollow centre. These academics are like blasé students who play the percentages, doing well in exams and essays by applying riskless techniques. They accumulate publications, but their success may mean less to them than others imagine.

Although collegiality and generosity exist in university corridors, the various scholarly examinations ensure that academic relations share the jealousy, seriality and *ressentiment* that lurk in student relations. These emotions are a reductive desire for sameness: academics often act as if in a zero-sum game where praise or reward for one person is praise or reward withheld from them. In such situations, they slyly police one another, sometimes taking pleasure in others' pain, sometimes undermining colleagues whose success or courage reflects badly on themselves, creating an environment where it is prudent to hide the joy you find in your own work.

While these disciplinary examinations involve objectification, scholars are also produced through subjectification, or self-discipline, the 'voluntary' internalisation of the criteria of judgement used in the scholarly community (see Foucault 1981: 57ff, 1982). The curriculum vitae is a major site for this self-objectification because it requires people to create inventories that transform the self into sets of fixed attributes with exchange-value. Exam results, publications, conference papers and the like become valuable as proof of such desirable qualities as scholarship, intelligence, experience and expertise. As the record of these examinatory marks on the academic's life, the CV is an object with which academics are morbidly preoccupied.

In sociology tea-rooms, people's CVs are discussed and measured, short ones dismissed quickly and long ones bringing forth treasured Anthony Giddens/Bryan Turner stories. In appointments committees, people's heads nod as they count publications. A colleague once complained about this reductionism while, out of habit, he too added up an applicant's score. At the privacy of their computer-screens, academics gloomily consider their own CVs. Is a long article worth several short ones? How many products (conference papers, working papers, articles, the book, the edited collection, the textbook, the second book) can be squeezed from a single project? Is it worth writing book reviews if they can't be included? Is the CV impressive enough yet to reapply for promotion? Is there a lull in the publishing strike rate that needs a special excuse? (As these questions suggest, teaching is seldom highly valued in academic CVs.)

In a double sense the CV is an account of a life, but this account isn't aimed only at an outside audience. Its construction involves concentrated introspection, and students and academics may well enjoy the self-indulgence of working and writing on themselves. Once the document is complete they have probably constructed an unusually coherent sense of who they are, and if they are persuaded by the CV's account, they have internalised the results of examination processes. Processes of subjectification may be involved even when people consciously falsify their CVs. Prudent academics and students who decide to exclude something negative from their CVs are choosing not to confess (out loud) to certain weaknesses, but they may have arrived at this decision through harsh judgements of their true qualities. In reflective moods, they may well accept and blame themselves for the 'inadequacies' in the 'true' CV that they and God witnessed.

The CV is easily internalised as a marker of self-worth because, like money, it is based on public and apparently objective measures. Many people fear that their sense of self-worth is delusion, and that the esteem in which they are held by others (family, friends, lovers) can be discounted because it arises from ignorance or obligatory love. The marks recorded on report cards are not tainted in these ways, and may even be sought because they promise objective distinction and definition.

The intense disciplinary regimes operating on academics are (too) similar to those they apply to students, involving the objectifications of examinations as well as the subjectifications that turn the discipline of sociology into the self-disciplines of the sociologist. Nevertheless, academics rarely concede the organisational embeddedness of their knowledges, preferring the security of imagining themselves as autonomous intellectuals committed to thought and truth, in the abstract. A professor I know likes to say that God didn't divide the world into disciplines. Perhaps, but we mortals cannot share God's abstracted perspective. We cannot simply escape our passionate relations with these profane institutions.

If students saw the anxiety behind the academic bluff, they might better appreciate the insecurities associated with university knowledge. If this stopped them blaming themselves for feeling vulnerable, and stopped them fantasising about the achievement of intellectual security, they might find better ways of managing the chronic tensions of academic work. Some determined undergraduates pursue this fantasy to postgraduate level, waiting for the degree that will release them from the weight of others' judgements, but there is no degree high enough.

* * *

While knowledges are always organisations and disciplines, many types of order can be generated, involving substantially different codes, rules, relations and knowledges. To investigate the order that presently dominates sociology, I will consider textbook sociology, and in particular the convention whereby textbooks describe the lives and thoughts of half a dozen or more 'founding fathers of sociology'. This comforting recitation isn't a description of sociology but a means of disciplining sociological teaching and research – a production of the rituals, confessions and terrors that provide a specific form of sociological identity and order. What ethical positions are implicit in the stories? What relations to truth, the world and the rest of society do they propose? What forms of writing, reading, teaching and learning do they authorise? What rites of passage do they impose on students? What relations do they establish between sociologists? What forms of knowledge do they help produce? And how might the discipline be socially and intellectually re-formed?

The textbook honour rolls do not celebrate writers, readers, teachers, mothers or parents. As the book titles of Coser (1971) and Raison (1979) proclaim, the commitment is to the idea of sociology's Masters and Fathers. Beatrice Webb is the only woman listed in the books I consulted, and she appears in her husband's shadow. As well as being patriarchal, the lists celebrate patrilineal descent: the image of the family tree is explicit on the cover of Abraham's *The Origins and Growth of Sociology* (1973) and in the lineage reproduced in Giddens' *Sociology* (1989: 702). This relentless recurrence of fatherly and familial metaphors *organises* both sociology and its story. The tropes establish sociology as a sexual order and an institution of generational power; they insist that, differences aside, sociologists constitute a family; they identify sociology's siblings and cousins and aunts; they allude to the imagined family get-togethers that create the ideal sociological community in a Durkheimian sense (see *Magic*); they demand filial love and loyalty; they act as if the family and patri-lineal forms were natural, and natural for sociology. Were these dubious moral claims and demands not embedded in the text-books, the seminal/paternal metaphors would be conspicuous rather than commonplace and sociologists would be forced to justify the particular institutional principles, social relations, eval-uative criteria and knowledges of founding fathers sociology. Instead the textbooks have no sociological curiosity about their own conventions.

Familial imagery turns sociology's politico-institutional story into a natural history, as fixed and obvious as kinship pretends to be, but the story remains unstable because it excludes the very maternal factor that biologically naturalises kinship. The found-ing fathers constitute an 'unnatural' chaste patriline, a discipline born of male leaders born of other men. Spurning nature's sexual difference, these chaste fathers take their cues from the pre-natural or divine, recalling the integrity of the God of Genesis and of celibate male priesthoods.

The religious stories underpinning sociology's patriarchal hon-our rolls are clear in the account of Comte, the founding father who named the discipline, who saw the sociologist as a form of father or priest. Comte believed that families and religion are two unifying forces essential in society. The basic social unit is the family and not the individual: 'It is by this avenue that Man comes forth from his mere personality, and learns to live in another, while obeying his most powerful instincts' (Comte 1973: 115). Religion, likewise, lets men transcend egoism in the love of their fellows, religious rites and beliefs unifying society (see Coser 1971: 11).

When Comte talked of Man coming forth through family units, he was thinking of the paterfamilias – the head of a household, someone who is his own Master. Such fathers *are* families. They are not simply immersed *in* families, like children or mothers; through mastering it they transcend and unify it. This explains how Comte can claim both that men are of families and that fam-ilies are the medium for Man's fulfilment. Families make Fathers of mere men, lifting them above the baseness of their mere per-sonality and allowing them to master their biosexual instincts.

Comte echoes St Paul: after priestly celibacy, marriage is the best way of mastering the dangers of passion and flesh. (Comte would therefore find this a very scandalous book.)

For Comte, the father is to the family as the sociologist is to society. While insisting that religion was essential to society, Comte argued that sociology was the last and most general of the positive sciences, the self-consciousness of progress, destined to replace the old religions. The Masters of Sociological Thought, Comte averred, would become the High Priests of Humanity, wielding scientific truths to create the harmony, justice and rectitude not provided by the Bible:

> The egoistic propensities to which mankind was prone throughout previous history would be replaced by altruism, by the command, *Live for others*. Individual men would . . . lovingly venerate the positivist engineers of the soul who in their wisdom would incarnate the scientific knowledge of man's past and present and the lawfully determined path into a predictable future. (Coser 1971: 13)

Through mastering families, men aspire to transcend mere personality and sexuality to become fathers, thereby embodying and transcending families. Through mastering society, sociologists reach higher again, transcending mere religion and sociality to become High Priests of Humanity. The founding fathers of sociology become priestly fathers of society. Not simply religious, they are priests and prophets; not simply social, they are scientists of the social; not simply immersed in society and religion, they are masters of society and religion.

Embarrassed by Comte's Mosaic ambitions, textbooks try to separate them from his real or scientific enterprise (e.g. Coser 1971: 13), but Comte insisted that science and religion are inextricable, the science starting from religion and returning to it in more encompassing form. The Mosaic ambition is not a deviation but a rigorous conclusion. When Abraham dismisses Comte's priestly themes as the *reductio ad absurdum* of his thought (1973: 89), he implicitly concedes that Comte's fault was to reveal the divine ambitions of sociologists aspiring to master and speak for society.

Most sociologists enjoy the common academic fantasy of knowledge as an illumination, revelation or discovery of pre-

existing truth. It is an apparently modest view, positioning sociologists as servants of Truth, but a servile relation to an external
Truth can set up social relations of prophetic authority. Comte
shows too clearly how power and religion can continue to operate through sociology, despite the claims that it is part of the
enlightenment project of unmasking power and supplanting religion and magic. The fervour of righteousness catching in their
throats, sociologists often offer themselves as the voice of Society,
the vanguard of History or the self-consciousness of Modernity,
able to identify objectively other people's interests and destiny,
and capable of standing outside the society they're in. This is a
priestly order, divine truth above sanctioning discipleship and
prophetic authority below.

The patriarchal model orders books like Coser's *Masters of
Sociological Thought* (1971). Coser augments an epigraph from
Goethe – 'What you have inherited from your fathers, acquire it
in order to possess it' – with relentless metaphors of mastery and
apprenticeship, choosing subheadings like 'The End of
Apprenticeship', 'Marx's Parental Background and Early
Companions', 'Gathering Disciples and Finding an Audience',
'In the Footsteps of Darwin and Spencer', 'In the Father's House',
'The Years of Mastery', 'The Sage of Ann Arbor'. He explains
that he wrote *Masters* after a discussion of Weber's value neu-
trality with a young male student. When the student made a
contemptuous gesture and accused Weber of 'copping out',
thereby positioning him as a political neuter, Coser was so out-
raged by the filial impiety that he set about teaching such
students a lesson. Explicitly set within an Oedipal struggle about
political potency and castration, Coser's textbook demands that
students respect the Masters' rightful authority. Whom, however,
is Coser defending? Is the Masters' authority precious because it
is the basis of his own?

* * *

In 1976, amidst attempts to eliminate their undergraduate pro-
gramme, anthropologists at New York's City University gathered
for a lecture series, 'Reconsidering the Ancestors', at which
anthropologists discussed an earlier generation of colleagues,
positioning themselves as students and the latter as teachers. The

lectures became a book, *Totems and Teachers*, which the authors dedicated to *their* students (Silverman 1981). Clearly, the seminar organisers understood that anthropology had its own totems, taboos and ancestor cults, but the contributors were remarkably silent about these themes, perhaps because their family was under threat. Robert Murphy alone developed the references to totemism and ancestor cults:

> It is a Durkheimian, and Freudian, maxim that the ancestors do live among us. . . . This has long been intuited among many peoples through the institutions of ancestor worship, which speak of the organic and continuing social and psychological links between the generations, links that symbolise the corporate nature of society. The ties between our anthropological teachers and founders and our-selves may not be as primary as those of kinship, but they are commonly modelled on these attachments and share some of their qualities. (1981: 173–4)

As far as they go, these are useful observations, but I'm curious about their timidity. If comparing anthropology and ancestor cults, why doesn't Murphy take the obvious next step, to consider the religious processes that constitute anthropology? By showing that we live amongst our ancestors, even as they live amongst us (see *Stories*), such a venture would correct his one-directional model of historical influence and allow Murphy and his collabo-rators to reflect more critically on their own role. Were they simply following in their parents' footsteps, or were they consti-tuting these to legitimate their own paths and discipline their own students? What anthropological understanding of anthro-pology are they offering?

Such questions arise as soon as anthropology's own totems and ancestors are considered from a Durkheimian perspective. While worshippers bow humbly before the awesome powers of totems, icons and idols, Durkheim insists that they originally gave the objects their power. Devotees acknowledge but mis-recognise their collective social power: they worship their own capacities. Aspects of this argument apply also to ancestor cults. As a standard account indicates, these cults convert the aura of ancestral spirits into the power of the priests and ritual specialists who claim to divine the ancestral will:

The ancestors rarely act on their own initiative; generally these avenging angels of justice are invoked by the local elder. . . . As the ancestor spirits are such realistic replicas of living elders it is perhaps not surprising that they should work in such close and harmonious collaboration. (Lewis 1976: 93)

If this standard account recognises that ancestors are shaped by those who speak for them in the present, Murphy's timidity must have arisen from his reluctance to question his own priestly position as elder and ancestral spokesman.

These comments on anthropological ancestors also apply to the founding fathers of other disciplines, as evident in Coser's wrath when his 'father' was challenged by his 'son'. They lead to a paradoxical conclusion. Founding fathers are mastered masters. Stories about the fathers initiate novices and maintain the traditions and totemic procedures by which sociologists recognise and celebrate their disciplinary identities. Founding fathers are sacred figures of patriarchal majesty. They are also, however, as pitiable as aged parents abused by their children. They are controlled, pigeon-holed, spoken for and misrepresented by the very people who proclaim their obeisance; they are powerless hostages forced to read the scripts of their captors. The mantle of sacred power they have to wear is an insult to their own work.

When the Freudian themes of *Totem and Taboo* (1960) are taken seriously, they too destabilise Murphy's account in *Totems and Teachers*. Regardless of its value as academic history, Freud's account draws attention to the grotesque mythic structures that underlie sociology's ancestral cult and authorise the relations of contract, authority, patriarchy and fraternity operating between sociologists (see Brown 1966; Pateman 1988).

Freud argues that the initial form of human society was a primal horde, in which a violent father kept all the women for himself and drove away his adult sons. Eventually the exiled brothers used their collective strength to kill the father, commemorating this ancient Oedipal murder in totemic rituals:

Cannibal savages . . . they devoured their victim as well as killing him. The violent primal father had doubtless been the feared and envied model of each one of the company of brothers: and in the act of devouring him they accomplished their identification with him, and each one of them acquired a portion of his strength. The totem

meal, which is perhaps mankind's earliest festival, would thus be a repetition and a commemoration of this memorable and criminal deed, which was the beginning of so many things – of social organisation, of moral restrictions and of religion. (1960: 142)

After the brothers enacted their hatred of the father, their love and respect for him arose as remorse and guilt, leading to such 'deferred obedience' as the ban on future killing of the totem, the father substitute. The brothers also renounced incestuous rights over women, thereby protecting their fraternal bonds from sexual jealousy. Moreover, in honouring the dead father, they reinforced their own authority over sons. As Freud remarks, 'The dead father became stronger than the living one had been. . . . What had up to then been prevented by his actual existence was thenceforward prohibited by the sons themselves' (1960: 143). Fraternity is thus based on a sexual contract between men brought together by their simultaneous rejection and adoration of a founding father.

This story goes far beyond Murphy's use of it, for it is specifically the *murdered* and *devoured* father who is honoured by the sons. Their elaborate courtesy is more than a recognition of a patriarch's sacredness, it is both a guilty acknowledgement of their violation and an attempt to ensure that they don't fall victim to internal rivalry and their own sons. This analysis reveals the deeply ambivalent character of the honour rolls common in sociology.

Feminist commentaries on Freud's story concentrate on its presumption of male power and its silence about women (e.g. Pateman 1988). Men's capacity to allocate women as a resource is presented as a natural or pre-political matter, and the conduct of particular sexual relations is treated as a non-political and discreetly private matter. Our account of sociology parallels these feminist commentaries, the masculinism of Freud's story also animating the textbooks' stories about founding fathers. If women are excluded from Freud's account, and if women and sex are the profanations excluded from the textbooks' priestly patrilines, the scandals excluded from the dominant textbook sociology are the everyday practices through which the discipline reproduces itself: the writing, reading, lecturing and storytelling, the textbooks, university departments and disciplinary rituals with which this book is interested. The fathers resemble Gods because they rise above such (womanly?) practices. Underlying sociology's silence is the fear that self-reflection may threaten the discipline's abstract, objective and universalist concerns; this is a dread of the particularity, narcissism and ineffectuality that Freud associated with femininity. Textbook sociology also fears the complexities of the reproductive encounter with difference; it mistrusts the uncontrollable difference of students and readers.

Sociologists use founding fathers to establish a safely distant Mosaic authority in relations with students. Sociology courses and texts on the founding fathers are transformative rites of passage, communions which incorporate novices into (a particular form of) the discipline by teaching them to incorporate and speak for the dead fathers. Conventional understandings see the reading and learning processes as acts of consumption rather than production: books are brain food, knowledge is stored in libraries, corpuses are devoured and bodies of knowledge are swallowed to absorb their power and allow later re-presentation through one's own mouth. Students adopt this gustatory model when cribbing or cramming for exams. A crib is a meal or a rack from which animals pull fodder, to crib is to plagiarise or copy. Students speak of regurgitating the founding fathers in exams and essays, and lecturers can grade these essays with pinpoint accuracy because their university and discipline have established their capacity to speak for the fathers. Given the mixed messages about plagiarism, the fear and guilt surrounding it at university are unsurprising.

While ostensibly honouring a past generation of writers, the honour rolls also produce forms of discipline and knowledge in the present. Ruthlessly denying the dead authors' right to difference, sociologists use them to establish and naturalise their own totemic solidarities, divisions and hierarchies: by putting all sociologists in identical relations to the fathers, this disciplinary order turns sociologists into brothers and gives sociology the moral coherence of a fraternity. This is the emotional communion that sociologists enter when adopting and recognising the 'proper' authorised form for theoretical arguments. These feelings of propriety sanctify sociology, giving a divine charter to a particular institutional order. The dark side of this inclusion is the punitive exclusion of other writers whose relations to the 'fathers' are considered improper. Such people can have trouble getting published, getting research funds, getting jobs; their subjects can be marginalised and students can be warned to avoid them.

If this patriarchal model of sociology is dominant, it isn't inevitable or ubiquitous. Sociology will always be ordered, but it can be ordered differently. It might, for example, think of sociologists as writers and readers, or teachers and students, or passionate partners, rather than fathers and children; it might celebrate rather than efface the discipline's creativity. It might recognise its own social and cultural forms; it might allow more interdisciplinary flow across its boundaries. It might admit its own pleasures and passions rather than adopting the passive–aggressive rhetoric of filial duty. Such changes in the rules of sociological scholarship would change sociological knowledge.

* * *

Knowledge is created through disciplinary tensions in particular institutional settings. While one might conceivably apologise for choosing to develop *sociological* knowledge, and while one should appreciate its specificity and partiality, it makes little sense to apologise for the institutionality of academic thought when institutionality makes it academic. What one can do, however, is play with the disciplinary rules and boundaries. There are always techniques for managing university that alter the forms of knowledge produced; there are always marginalised knowledges that can unsettle the complacent conventions of the centre; it's always possible to pursue the rules of academic knowledge production further than normal, to challenge and change these rules. These are the processes to which this book is dedicated. The way we practise sociology institutionally changes the discipline, endlessly creating new possibilities.

Managing

*If I read this sentence, this story, or this word with pleasure,
it is because they were written in pleasure. (Barthes 1975: 4)*

While many academics would chide Barthes for the self-indulgence of his call to pleasure, we think students and teachers of
sociology should insist on writing and reading for pleasure. If we
cannot eliminate institutionality, we *can* create spaces for alternative and pleasurable forms of reading and writing. It is a matter of
how creatively we *manage*.

Managing has connotations of discipline and organisation, and
also of coping. There are many ways in which we manage – cope
with – academic life, but while some strategies replicate the standard principles of the institution, managing can also involve
creative strategies that challenge normalisation, quantification
and the disciplinary rules and forms of knowledge. Put more
positively, any challenge to prevailing institutional forms and
rules requires management, shifting or playing with the rules
being a form of creative management. And if we value pleasure
(surprising, delighting, moving, disturbing pleasure, not just
comfortable, easy pleasure), creative management might itself
constitute that pleasure. This conception of managing brings discipline and pleasure into close alignment; in combination they
move us beyond *just* managing.

Although evaluation is one of the most imperious demands of
universities, even it can be managed. Teachers have the greatest
opportunity to shift the processes and criteria of evaluation, but
students who read and write for pleasure also creatively subvert
the institutional principles of assessment and normalisation. By
making the thrill of disruptive pleasure a criterion of evaluation,
you can change the experiences of reading and writing. We'll

make the point by looking at ways of managing a piece of written research.

* * *

Let us begin with two uncreative ways of coping with institutional pressures. Boredom and a blasé attitude are common forms of self-managements in academic life, akin to the psychic responses of reserve, intellectuality and blasé attitude that Simmel (1950) associated with metropolitan life. Boredom and a blasé attitude manage the academic world of grades and timetables by adopting its qualities, reducing qualitative differences to quantifications and abstractions, and privileging the intellect over the emotions. They are forms of self-constitution and self-management that accommodate people to universities.

Boredom isn't simple, Barthes remarked (1975: 25), and he demonstrated its complexity by offering apparently divergent accounts. In one place he wrote that 'to be bored means one cannot produce the text, play it, release it, *make it go*' (1986: 63), but elsewhere he insisted that boredom is never sincere and never far from bliss: 'it is bliss seen from the shores of pleasure' (1975: 25-6). Where the first account emphasises the prohibition of play, the second highlights an unwillingness to play. This discrepancy suggests that bored university students may be either barred from play or refusing to play. In Simmel's term (1950: 409ff), the second form of self-management involves a blasé attitude.

Universities frequently prohibit play. Lectures are often designed not to stimulate or exemplify, but as Luddite demonstrations of how 'the main points' can be accurately conveyed from the lecturer's notes to the student's notepad without the use of a photocopier. Most textbooks reduce play further by insisting that they provide a matter of fact transparency. On this model of knowledge and communication, students' creativity should be strenuously avoided, as noise, deviation, error. And while students cannot avoid playing with even the most prohibitive lectures and textbooks, few enjoy the institutional freedom to *revel* in this play, as famous academics like Barthes and Derrida might. When caught between the authoritarian clarity of lectures and textbooks and the clear testing processes of the grade, students feel a drudgery and anxiety that disengage them from their own involvement in university. While doing what's required, they protect their dignity by splitting who they are from what they do. This boredom is a not insincere way of coping with university, but it offers little challenge to the institutional order.

If enforced passivity generates boredom, blasé attitudes are an insincere boredom used to shield a fantasy of stable individuality from the destabilising effect of too many stimuli and possibilities. If boredom responds to university at its worst, blasé attitudes may be a defence against university at its confronting best. University can suddenly remove the ground rules of your school life; instead of being a disinterested consumer of knowledge, you're expected to engage actively in new knowledge games you don't understand; you're assailed with new ideas that threaten the fantasies of self you bring to university and which you think of *as* yourself; lost in the labyrinth of the library and bureaucracy and the vastness of the campus, alone and lonely in the crowds, you hope no-one will insult you with pity; your panic rises as familiar words empty themselves of meaning, and with a cold and dreadful certainty you know you're the only one really having trouble.

These challenges may not be relentless or uniformly negative, but nightmare still shadows the best university experiences, and one way of coping with it is to produce yourself as blasé. While ideas swirl around them, blasé students stay cool, reserved, cynical, apparently confident that nothing matters more than the lasting security of the degree itself. Treating university time as money, they resent ambiguity and demand clarity, reducing what they study to points that will be useful and easily accommodated. If their refusal of university's ecstatic possibilities arises from a resentful unwillingness to relinquish the control and methods that previously brought high grades, blasé students may feel a latent antipathy to people who *do* find something thrilling and valuable in university life. Desiring what they dare not have, they become entangled in the deathly coils of envy.

Not only does the precious stability of the blasé self become a prison, its self-defence is ultimately self-destructive, 'devaluating the whole objective world . . . which in the end unavoidably drags one's own personality down into a feeling of the same worthlessness' (Simmel 1950: 411). Students with blasé attitudes can take no real thrill in their own qualities at university, because they know they didn't really display or explore these qualities. A blasé essay might accumulate good marks, particularly if it 'answers' a fixed essay question, but as a riskless exercise in ventriloquism it won't open possibilities for future work or provide an encouraging affirmation of one's rich capacities.

The blasé attitude is at least as common among academics as students. Like most disciplines, sociology has itself been blasé, refusing to analyse the emotionality of its own intellectuality, squirming to avoid the shocks of the most vital social experiences – like love, grace, communion, mortality, corporeality, awe, wonder, pain, passion, violence. Sociology usually prefers to deal with such experiences when abstraction has disarmed them and accommodated them within familiar meta-narratives about capitalism, patriarchy, modernity, rationalisation and so on. Just as a blasé essay provides *the* answer, academics provide *the* ready-made explanation. The institutional structures that generate blasé attitudes also generate blasé knowledges.

* * *

Boredom and the blasé attitude are ways of coping with the institutional demands of university, but it is also possible to manage without repressing creativity, joy, emotional intensity and pleasure in difference. Much depends on what we teachers and students *do* with the institutional regimes around us. Here is the story of how one of us developed a creative form of managing:

I learned my most valuable undergraduate lesson in a subject to which I was committed only by curiosity. In my third year at university, wanting a break from full-time studies, I enrolled in just one subject, a history subject on Victorian England. To my delight I found that I approached the essays in this subject in a lighter, more joyous mood than I normally experienced. Because my primary commitments elsewhere reduced the penetration of the examiner's gaze, the essays were adventures in which I had nothing to lose. I remained aware of a readership, but I imagined it as a sympathetic readership, made up of people somewhat like me.

Even though I was writing assessable essays mediated through essay-writing conventions, I felt like an historian setting my own agenda. For pleasure, I advanced what I thought were extremely brave and idiosyncratic arguments. I still recall the physical pleasures of the experience – the excitement of hunting around the library, the almost tangible air of self-absorbed con-templation, the fearful thrill of pushing the ideas beyond what I thought was their proper domain, the satisfaction of the words falling into place, the sensuality of the performance of self (surely there is an element of showing off in all writing). I recall too my unbearable impatience awaiting the lecturer's response. Although I've never spoken to this lecturer, or wanted to, I wanted his comments as urgently as someone wanting a response to an audacious Valentine's Day card. I wasn't so much seeking judgement as proof that my work had had the effect on readers that I desired.

This experience became my model for academic reading and writing. I was unwilling to relinquish these pleasures when I returned to full-time studies, and they still guide my research life. A good day's writing is a joyous self-indulgence that I refuse to do without. It makes me feel alive, concentrated, invin-cible.

While the thrill of writing is its own reward, important benefits accompany it. If writing for my own pleasure, I can longer delay the deadening effects of examination processes. I will have worked on myself to produce a body without fear, or even aware-ness, of an examiner's eyes. Examinations will come, of course, but by then the writing will be done. Moreover, because the examination is no longer the purpose of writing, by the time it comes it will have lost its unanswerable authority. Although most lecturers appreciated the essays I wrote through these self-disci-plines, I wasn't devastated by the couple who didn't. Feeling spurned but intact, I was more likely to uphold my position in an imaginary debate with them; instead of telling me I was 'wrong', their red ink had to pass tests of my own.

The joy of good writing days doesn't eliminate the devastating experience of bad days, and these may be as blackly depressing as the others are exhilarating (it's hard to say because good days bring a lovely amnesia and I'm writing this on a good day). Nevertheless, I've developed ways of coping when the words are sullen, when the possibility of hope seems absurd, when examination processes creep into my study and pronounce me a failure, when I'm only surprised it has taken people so long to discover that I'm a fraud.

I've found it important to become familiar with the qualities of black days, in the way children learn to know and perhaps even befriend the night. I've become observant about the moods involved, when they arise, the forms they take, how long they last, and I can often recognise the patterns as they occur. Now that I understand them, I'm less afraid of my own fear; dealing with blockages becomes a matter of patience and resilience – and management. Black days are never welcome, but because I'm sure I'll never entirely escape them, no matter how many degrees I have, no matter how much I publish, I've had to come to working arrangements with them.

Sometimes the best way to deal with my writer's block is to luxuriate in gloom for a while, perhaps in a long bath or perhaps hiding in bed. Sometimes the writer's block is prolonged by fighting it, for I'm left divided between the depression and the self-loathing I feel for allowing myself to become blocked and depressed.

At other times, though, I force myself to sit at the word-processor and work my way through to the other side of the block. This strategy requires me to keep writing even when its hollowness disgusts me and my lack of confidence terrifies me. What I write matters less than that I write. It may be better to circle around the place where I became stuck than to sit at the empty screen until I finally see my way to the proper path. Even if I later decide I've written several irrelevant pages, they've probably worked their way to the path they should have been taking, and looking back from this intersection I can often see where my writing originally went astray. Moreover, the deviation has probably uncovered ideas useful elsewhere in the project.

Whether I temporarily give in to my gloom, or work my way through it, it is most important that I remember that writing isn't always like this. Black days may be a necessary part of the writing life, but I find great reassurance in knowing I've managed to survive these things before.

What is striking about this account is the passion: managing writing involves an acknowledgement of the complex, and sometimes painful, emotions involved. More than this, the account suggests that research can be creatively managed by writing with emotion and for pleasure. Furthermore, there are clearly disciplines and self-disciplines involved in this pleasure.

* * *

For whom do we write? Working on the writing self revolves around this complex question and its corollaries: What does it mean to write for your own pleasure? What relation to readers does this imply? Does it produce writing careless of its readers? Is it possible to write simultaneously for your self and for an other?

At its simplest, the notion of writing for myself might mean that my writing pays no regard to readers and is designed only to please my writing self. This approach to writing can be an effective short-term strategy for managing the writing self. By reducing my fear of readers, reassuring me that no-one else will ever read what I'm writing, it can help me produce a first draft to bridge the awful emptiness of the blank page, to produce a text to work with. More specifically, it allows much of the writing to be done before it is imagined from the position of particularly fearsome readers – examiners, book reviewers, hostile colleagues.

But although I can effectively tell myself that I don't care about readers, this strategy almost inevitably relies on an unsustainably solipsistic fantasy. When I write for my own pleasure, I am also writing for readers, even if the imagined reader is another aspect of my self. Writing and reading are not separate processes, for we read when we write just as we listen when we speak, just as we watch when we work with our hands, and it is through this reading, listening and watching that we monitor and adjust – organise – our work. Moreover, when I write I am aware of the sort of writing that I like as a reader. I write to meet my own desires as a reader by imagining myself as a particular type of reader, and I address these desires by striving for the stylistic codes that will not only tell me how to read the text but will bring me reading pleasure. This is an uncertain process. I may love what I'm writing while the words are flowing yet loathe it when

I read it. This is the gap between the writing and reading self. In short, all writing assumes imagined readers and all reading assumes imagined writers, and the writing and reading selves slide in and out of alignment.

This point is neatly made by thinking about private diary entries, which are often addressed to 'Dear Diary' and which always embody assumptions about the Diary's expectations as a reader. Likewise, when I write letters I address imagined readers ('Dear X') and specify my relation and attitude to that reader ('Your loving friend, A'). Each letter varies with the character of the relationship, as does the writing body and the psychic discipline through which it works. My subjectivity and writing will change again when I write a promotion application, a journal article or a book like this.

If writing for pleasure rarely involves a denial of a readership, it does depend on the particular relations between the writer and the imagined reader. Institutional rules and protocols often restrict the relations that can be adopted, and we often augment the restrictions by imagining these institutional forms as more severe than they are, but I find it's even possible to enjoy writing bureaucratic reports if I focus on the technical craft of skilful self-presentation. Fortunately, however, sociological writing is rarely as constrained as this. One of the discipline's charms is its diversity. Whatever the orthodox position, it is always possible to imagine readers you can respect and trust, readers who excite you with the desire to take risks and push arguments. These are the readers whom you probably invest with the attributes that you aspire to as reader and writer. Like many imagined lovers, they seem to resemble you, only more so, allowing you to imagine yourself at your best.

Writing for an imagined readership that you trust and respect is the source of the deepest writing pleasures, because it allows the fullest testing of your writing capacities, the freshest and most honest arguments, the least bluff, defence and ventriloquism, the most play, the least condescension. Writing to a trusted reader is not a statement from the dock but an invitation to a dance, offering a sympathetic partner the chance to play with your text, to hear its harmonies, to note its dissonances, to make it part of their own experience, to put it in motion, to realise its possibilities. Living apart but in anticipation, trusting writers and readers complete each other. It is a very generous and passionate relation.

Writing for pleasure is not, therefore, a selfish act, any more than dancing for pleasure is. It involves a celebration of a relation of trust and intimacy with the reader. Writing that is a joy to read has probably been written for the writer's pleasure, but with a desire for the desire of the other. Such writing produces a text that respectfully allows the reader the same play and joy that it gave the writer.

Students' writing changes when they stop writing to the imagined requirements of the Fathers and guardians of academic law. Because they are now thinking–writing for themselves, in every sense, their writing feels alive with the pleasure in ideas and intellectual discipline. This life gives their writing a distinctive *voice* – a *living* of intellectual practice transmitted in the writing – and this is what we look for in students' work. Once students believe in their ability to think and write creatively, when they are no longer *burdened* by institutional rules, a supple lightness can develop in their writing: a subtle and nuanced writing that allows tensions to remain, a writing that sings and surprises and disturbs. These qualities won't be to everyone's taste, but for us they are crucial to a pleasurable writing–reading, and by valuing them we try to change the meaning of the examination process in which we and students are implicated.

Perhaps because sociologists often study cruelty of one sort or another, they've traditionally been uneasy about the pursuit of pleasurable writing, treating writing as perfunctory duty, a form of 'writing up' to be judged in utilitarian terms. Sociology fears that the seriousness of its enterprise is compromised by pleasure in its practice. This book insists that this attitude is based on a sociologically naive understanding of cultural production. Not only is a dutifully earnest tone no guarantee that sociologists are respecting the seriousness of their studies, it dampens the emotional and intellectual effects of sociology and keeps its implications at a safely abstract distance. Dutiful writing is as condescending and perversely comforting as the tone of television newsreaders giving their nightly catalogue of the world's wars and disasters. To have cruelty's measure, sociological writing must break through the conventional forms of representation rather than turning them into proofs of sincerity.

We make no apologies, then, for valuing the joyous self-indulgence in a good day's writing. Not only can writing be an enormously self-affirming experience, one needs a positive relation with the self to write well. Narcissism perhaps? Writers like Freud who have disparaged narcissism have used the term in relation to quite disparate psychic phenomena. We would like to refigure some forms of narcissism in a positive way, paralleling our account of writing for pleasure – a writing for the self that is simultaneously a writing for the other. Does not Narcissus' drowning in the desire for identity invite a redemption in terms of difference? While narcissism can take the form of closed self-love, it can also take more creative forms. Indeed a marked degree of self-esteem and self-reflection are preconditions for loving, generous and trusting self–other relations. Thus, to write for the other requires a form of self-care.

Consider the different forms of selfhood involved in the blasé attitude and narcissism. Seeking stability, boundedness and singularity, the blasé self wants writing to provide the reassurance of the single answer and the safety of abstractions that protect its fantastic stability. By contrast, narcissism, as we are refiguring it, is a form of relation with the self that acknowledges difference. Understanding the self as forever incomplete and always changing, it also understands the incompleteness of knowledge, and here lies its potential for creativity. To write is to open up and be open to possibilities for creation and self-creation in the world. Writing for oneself is a writing for the other in oneself. Nietzsche's description of the self-affirming artist captures this well: 'everything that he is not yet, becomes for him an occasion of joy in himself' (1976: 519). The creativity of narcissism comes of a 'not yet' arriving at oneself, a permanent becoming.

Narcissism, then, is a technique of self-management. This Foucaultian idea is particularly apt when the self is understood to be in process: discipline of the self is intimately connected with a creation of the self. When being is a becoming, the emphasis is on *self*-discipline; the imposition of an external order of conduct won't work if we are to be open to change and potentiality in the self. In *Twilight of the Idols* Nietzsche argues that passion needs and is needed by asceticism or self-moderation. Together they are the basis of life and creativity (1976: 486–8).

* * *

Knowledge practices are practical matters. Thinking, speaking, reading and writing are skills that must be learned and practised (Nietzsche 1976: 571-3); a piece of writing is a task of work requiring management of time, space, knowledge, concepts, moods, rhythms, rituals, words and word-processors. Throughout this book we emphasise the materiality of knowledge practices as a counter to the widespread mystification of knowledge and genius, for this mystique ultimately incapacitates most students under its thrall. So invested in 'the essay' or 'the thesis' do they become, so burdened with notions of genius, so oppressed by a duty of earnestness, that they are paralysed by anticipations of their own inadequacy. Such an experience of writing is far from pleasurable.

Creativity and a passion for knowledge aren't destroyed by attention given to the practices of intellectual life. The organisation of practice can produce spaces and opportunities for passionate intellectual engagement. Here, as an example, we consider 'the proposal' as one stage in the overall organisation of a lengthy piece of writing.

The proposal is a valuable technique for getting a project started and framed, giving writers an opportunity to truly identify their interests and desires. While most writers are led to the broad areas of their research by personal obsessions and intuitions, it can be difficult and painful to identify these precisely, without bluff or duty, and to turn them into a viable topic, especially if the writer hasn't developed a comfortable voice for performing sociology. The proposal is an exercise to clarify and fill out the academic voice, strengthening it with the body and stamina of the writer's preoccupations and feelings. The ability to produce an interesting and coherent proposal also serves as a useful preliminary test of the project's viability, worth and conceptual adequacy; a proposal allows the researcher–writer to seek advice from others, to persuade tutors, funding bodies, publishers and supervisors that the project deserves support, and to redirect and reassure themselves when feeling lost. Finally, the completed proposal helps the researcher–writer decide what tasks must be done when.

As the term suggests, a proposal is a partially public document. We are making a proposal to . . ., inviting an audience to join us. This sense of putting yourself on the line often produces fear, symptomatic of the more general fear that comes from knowing that we *are* writing for an audience: that our work will ultimately be separated from us and that we will then lose control over the part of us invested in our 'baby'. One of the strengths of the proposal, however, is that it is a preliminary document, for discussion, for trying out ideas, which need only be shown at first to people we trust, and which leaves open opportunities for change. Regarding the thesis or book or essay as a series of limited tasks like this is a way of gradually overcoming the fear of audience and the writing blocks that ensue. It creates a space for experimentation.

The usefulness of the book, thesis or research proposal depends on its potential for flexibility. It should remain a provisional intellectual itinerary because we can't foretell the issues and options that will emerge during research–writing and a proposal shouldn't obstruct our exploration of them. If we do deviate from the original proposal, it will still have helped us get started and organised; it will have provided the path we need in order to wander. Moreover, we may even remain satisfied with our pre-planning when journeying forth.

There is no fixed format for a proposal, so take the following outline as a starting point to play with. The most common structure has two parts: an introductory blurb of at least a paragraph and at most two pages, and a brief description of each chapter. It should be written with economy and simplicity, so that it is accessible to people without expertise in the field. This double demand is often a stumbling block, economy leading to a denseness in the writing, but it is important that each sentence follow, that different points are separated, that connections between points are presented, that what might seem obvious is said.

The introduction is a framing exercise, setting up the question with which the proposed project is concerned. 'The question' is what students have most difficulty with. It is not something to which you will have an answer; it is a formulation of an issue, which may change during the production of the thesis, and which will certainly be elaborated. It is a puzzle ('Might it be that . . .?') which moves beyond a list of topics (e.g. 'My thesis is *about* . . . sociology, grunge, post-structuralism, mothers . . . .'). Topics are only the fields through which a thesis pursues its question (and at one level it usually is a single question). Formulating a question requires a reflexive identification of the motivations underlying your research. In the process of articulating why this research area engages you and provokes your desire for knowledge, you will already be formulating the question.

The introductory remarks might begin with a brief account of the phenomenon with which you're interested, using it as a setting for your question: 'This story raises important issues about. . . .' By involving readers experientially in your story, you engage them as you draw from your example the philosophical, theoretical and conceptual issues of interest to you. The abstract ideas come to life. You need to articulate the ways in which your concerns are connected, and what is significant about these connections.

Imagine, for example, writing a book or thesis 'about' sociology. Here is a possible beginning:

> Despite the common use of the term 'reflexive', sociology normally refuses to analyse its own practices sociologically. It is happier to view itself in terms of the history of ideas, a perspective that implies a spirit at work in sociology, guiding it ever closer to its destiny. *Passionate Sociology*, however, sees sociological knowledge as a cultural production that should be analysed like other cultural productions. We are therefore primarily concerned with the materiality of everyday practices that constitute sociological knowledge and the mediations through which these practices operate. . . . Instead of seeing knowledge in representational terms, *Passionate Sociology* insists on its productive character. Such an insistence has profound implications for the way in which sociology is imagined, altering our understandings of how sociology should be practised and evaluated.

'The question' in this instance might be: 'What are the implications of a passionate and productive conception of knowledge for sociological practice?' This could be spelled out in a paragraph, a chapter, a book.

The introduction invites readers to consider how provocative and important this question is. Here are examples:

> Our book's title seems at first a contradiction in terms, but we will explore what happens in putting passion and sociology together.
> Textbooks are extremely powerful tools within disciplinary

regimes. Their form of address positions students in particular power relations, normally as novices or apprentices who must learn the thoughts of the masters before potentially qualifying to practise as sociologists. Such a relation legitimates existing practices, mythologises past sociologists, gives apostolic authority to lecturers and textbook writers, and disempowers the students. Yet textbooks continually reproduce this model without reflecting on the ethics of such power relations.

An examination of sociology's practices and mediations not only provides students with an excellent introduction to the discipline, it simultaneously challenges the power relations normally implied in textbooks. *Passionate Sociology* is a subversion of the genre of 'the introductory textbook'.

The second part of the proposal specifies how each chapter will address the question, explaining how the particular questions to be asked will contribute to the broader question. This constitutes an itinerary. What are the various topics to be considered and how does each relate to central themes in the thesis or book? What aspects of the themes do the different topics highlight? In what order will you consider topics, or place chapters? Although the journey taken may diverge from the journey planned, it is still important to think carefully about the significance of different possible orderings of topics and treatments of themes. How will the work's meaning change if you take this direction or if you go here before there? Bear in mind the different temporalities operating here: plans order ideas within an imagined completed text, but because writers rarely work their way from first chapter to last, they rely on plans to maintain their sense of place and order.

An enjoyable part of planning is the selection of an overall title, chapter titles and possibly section titles. Titles are extremely helpful in the clarification and organisation of ideas, even if subheadings are removed after the first draft. We choose titles according to the symmetry and elegance of the work's structure and content, and find an aesthetic sense of fit and depth one of the main pleasures of planning and the major test of its success. Sociology must work as art, an artful title knowing more than the writer about the meanings of the text. Accordingly we avoid the imbalance of having some titles indicating 'theory' and others 'empirical content' – 'Foucault's theory of power' and 'grunge as resistance' – preferring titles that are commensurate with each other, highlighting structural patterns that entice readers and writers with movement, rhythm and a promise of beauty. We have tried to create such rhythms in this book's chapter titles: Passion, School, Managing, Magic, Stories, Writing, Ink, Reading, Desire, Knowing.

In writing each chapter description, explain how it addresses the framing question. The proposal shouldn't simply list what might go in the chapter. Here are two examples from the proposal for the book or thesis on sociology:

Stories

The chapter begins with a small treasury of stories of beginnings and goes on to explore their narrative structure: their religious character, their denial of time and change, the ritual significance of repetition. Stories are a way of organising knowledge but they are constitutive rather than descriptive. The chapter then uses these arguments to look more closely at the (sacred) stories sociology tells its novices about its own development. This explains why this book is refusing the normal 'what is sociology?' question and the normal approaches to introducing the discipline. The chapter ends by considering the masculinity, the fetishised authority and the sacrificial consumption of the discipline's founding fathers. This will lead into later discussions of authority and desire and knowledge.

Writing

It is curious that reading and writing are seldom discussed by sociologists even though they are central to a sociological labour process. This chapter takes up issues about different forms of writing, including writing that denies itself. It will address the ways in which writing and thought are inseparable, in connection with quite practical issues about 'how to write' and philosophical issues about writing. By moving between the practice of writing in a literal sense and metaphors for writing and the writer (and metaphors of writing, although there will be more of this in *Reading*), the very distinction between the literal and the metaphoric – implicit in sociological assumptions about writing – will be put into question. Contemporary notions of writing the body will be discussed in connection with the practice of writing, issues about the relation between the body and metaphor, and the relation of the self to writing.

This description of *Writing* ends with a list of topics that should be worked in, somehow; the 'how' is deferred to the process of writing. In the event some of the topics have been dropped. At the first draft stage *Stories* became two chapters, *Stories* and *Fathers*. At a later stage *Fathers* disappeared and pieces of it were relocated in other chapters, including *Stories*.

This discussion suggests how we have used the device of the proposal to manage our own work. The structure of a thesis or book usually changes in the process of writing, but without a plan it is difficult to start or sustain that process. We both keep the proposal beside us as we write, and the enormous enjoyment and creativity we've experienced in our collaboration wouldn't be possible without it.

* * *

The proposal is only one moment in the organisation of a piece of writing. Before the proposal a certain momentum of ideas is necessary; after the proposal come the drafts, the temporality and function of the first differing from the subsequent drafts written in the light of a 'whole' text before us; and on the way, there are the lists, the files and the piles on the desk that help us spatially organise our thinking–writing. Once we acknowledge that thinking and writing don't happen in single inspirational flashes, it becomes clear that these organisational issues are far from trivial. They invite creativity and should themselves be a source of sensual craft pleasure. It is important to find the way of working that works for you, but self-disciplines are crucial to the management of a piece of writing and to the possibility of pleasurable writing–reading. They allow writers to work creatively in institutional settings, avoiding the half-lives of boredom and a blasé attitude.

This chapter has worked from the claim that sociologists should consider their own work sociologically. This self-knowledge cannot provide a conscious mastery over the academic life but it may point to more open and productive working methods. We have concentrated here on managing the pleasure of writing, but later chapters range over other aspects of sociological production. By investigating the metaphors, stories, writing, literacy, reading and teaching relations on which sociology relies, we will suggest creative ways of managing the discipline's cultural forms and practices.

We are too down to earth to pursue a pure or abstract freedom through this book. We cannot escape the cultural forms in which we work and live. But we *can* enjoy the possibility of creatively managing our relations to these forms.

Magic

poetry is the guts of existence, every inner voice of every per-
son reading this speaks and breathes poetry – even as your
outer voice, your cool late-twentieth-century voice despises
and dismisses it. Your blood beats in metre, ladies and gen-
tlemen. (Porter 1994: 53)

Magic is alive in the play of metaphor and in the rituals that rely
on it. Although often dismissed as poetic affectation, metaphor is
actually the stuff of human life, constituting us in our most
abstract sciences as in our most ordinary practices. We live and
breathe the magic of poetry. Its pulse is the rhythm of our lives, its
metaphor the source of cultural creativity; it moves us, it becomes
us, it lets us act in the world.

As major constituents of sociology, and as conceptual bases
for our sociological analyses of sociology, metaphor and ritual are
central concerns of this book. This chapter is devoted to exploring
their character and significance. While alluding to the magical
qualities of sociology as a form of knowledge and a type of discipline, the chapter's main aim is to evoke the mystery generated in
everyday life by our reliance on metaphor and other tropes,
demonstrating the creative interplay between knowledge, passion, sensuality, poetry, performance and actuality. Other chapters
use these ideas to consider the everyday practices of sociology in
particular.

* * *

There is no non-metaphorical standpoint from which one could look
upon metaphor, and all the other figures for that matter, as if they

were a game played before one's eyes. In many respects, the continuation of this study will be a prolonged battle with this paradox.
(Ricoeur 1986: 18)

Appropriately, the word 'poetry' is itself unavoidably poetic,
alluding more or less resonantly to the term's Greek roots, *poiesis*
(creation, making, poem) and *poiein* (to make, do, create, com-
pose), while allowing the particular form, the poem, to function
as a synecdoche for creative production in general. Celebrating
language's capacity to *make* sense, poetry plays with the play in
language, metaphorising, punning, alluding, evoking, imagining, feigning, capturing, dreaming, slipping, echoing, yelling,
whispering, crying, singing, beating, pulsing, sounding. Because
the poets' materials vastly overrun their own capacity for com-
prehension and control, poetry gives a shockingly vagrant
understanding of experience, insisting that the things of our
world are not only not as they seem, but not simply where or
when or as they are. As the nomadic quality of its own meaning
suggests, poetry challenges fixed boundaries and territories.

It is not poetry but the poem that is prose's opposite, for all
prose has poetic qualities, which may bloom in the sparest prose,
and wither in the most 'purple' prose. When prose denies its
poetry it is poetically promising a plain-speaking literal language,
and this is the form of prose on which most sociology uncritically
relies. Its realism is its poetry. Fearing metaphor's capacity to
shift the ground under their claims to truth and self-certainty,
academics treat it not as the condition of language and knowledge but as an occasional and implicitly feminine adornment to
the expression of pre-existing meaning.

The view of metaphor as adornment assumes that it lends
one thing's name to something else, so that returning proper
names restores the literal truth (Aristotle 1941: 1476). On the
assumptions that employers are really humans, who really talk,
the metaphorical claim 'My boss growled at me' may literally
mean 'My boss talked angrily at me'. Literal language claims to
re-present external reality, using words whose meanings comes
from the things they name rather than the play of language.
Before showing how this misunderstands metaphor and knowledge, and diminishes sociology, I want to show it as an
antiseptic and fundamentalist fantasy. As Ricoeur insists, there

is no non-metaphorical standpoint, on language or the world.

Although dictionaries are often treated as guarantors of literal meanings, lexicography has no privileged access to real meanings and can only codify the patterns of meaning it generates by juxtaposing each word's usages. In short, it adopts the same metaphorical process that I unsystematically use when making sense of the growling shared by bosses, bears and lions. Given this inability to distinguish directly the figurative and literal, lexicographers rely on relative conventionality to identify the usages to be honoured with dictionary entries. Dictionaries are catalogues of partly forgotten and congealed metaphors, changing as usages become more or less conventional.

Consider the sociological term 'class struggle'. People may have once treated class struggle metaphorically, but familiarity has introduced it into dictionaries, lent it the self-certainty of the literal, and led sociologists to search in vain for the real thing it names. Nevertheless, the term's meaning is still produced metaphorically, even if much of the production occurs out of sight, in the computers of the lexicographers. Whatever class struggle means, it means because lamplight struggles through the darkness, because armies struggle in battle, because Christ struggled against temptation, because weight-lifters struggle with the bar-bell, and because evil struggles against good. Its meaning comes from the metaphorical processes linking these various domains.

While dictionaries *fix* metaphor to produce definitions, and while the usage of words is further entrenched by the dictionary usages themselves, dictionaries cannot stop the play of metaphor. Metaphorical processes allow dictionary users to apply listed meanings to their particular context, and every usage potentially creates new metaphorical possibilities. Dictionaries are constantly updated because words hybridise when moved to foreign domains.

Just as the metaphorical shocks of class struggle and the boss's growl are fading, an etymological dictionary reveals that 'literal' is usually a bleached metaphor, derived from usages that imply we can re-present the world as we can follow the letter(s) of God's words in the Bible. When used 'literally', the literal seems to carry a complex metaphoric understanding of the world as a text. At other times, however, 'literally' involves a lively metaphor, perversely implying 'metaphorically' ('I was so ashamed I literally died'). While usage guidebooks fulminate against this usage, dictionaries register it with a magnificent imperturbability, defining 'literally' both as 'really' and 'virtually'. Plain speaking plainly hasn't cut itself free of complexity, creativity and metaphor. It just refuses to acknowledge them.

These observations on metaphor's persistence can be augmented by noting the importance of poetic inflections often unrecorded in dictionary definitions. Even *if* words had literal meanings, they'd still carry connotations as traces of their history. If 'bourgeois' denotes 'capitalist', it also suggests complacent conventionality; class struggle always suggests war. Calling connotations myths, Barthes (1973: 158) remarked that facts and myths co-exist, with the fact acting as the myth's alibi, allowing writers to deny the full play of meaning in their texts. Industrial cities are polluted but, given existing linguistic usages, sociological references to industrial pollution always invoke a poetic underplay of purity, danger and dark satanic mills. The facts writers intend to convey are not the only meaning they generate.

It's also important to appreciate that the meanings of words vary with context. A lyricist's tree is not a horticulturalist's; a forest last century is not a forest this century. Not fixed by or within individual words, meaning is a 'social' relation scattered through the text and the contexts readers bring to it. Consequently, a final settlement of meaning must be continually deferred: even writers who strive for plain language word by word cannot control the reverberations created by the juxtapositions of different parts of their text or of their text and the contexts supplied by particular readers. Meanings can always migrate.

Finally, the poetry of academic prose is evident in the tropes that put the 'facts' of sociological evidence to work. Sociological writing figuratively implies more than it admits because even the longest ethnography couldn't offer a full account of even the shortest social interaction – and because it would in any case remain a text and not the interaction. The empirical material presented in sociological texts is not a presentation of the raw world but a rhetorical manoeuvre encouraging readers to accept the texts' plausibility and authenticity. It operates like period furniture in realist theatre, to reassure us rhetorically that we are facing the world directly, without the deceit of rhetoric.

Metonymy, for example, operates through contiguity or contagion, so that the crown signifies the queen it touches; synecdoche
allows substitutions between parts and wholes, so that the face
signifies the person of whom it is part. Such tropes turn water
into wine and the driest and most 'literal' sociological analyses
into a poetry that plays simultaneously at a range of levels of
meaning. Because it is impossible to specify exhaustively what
connects with or is part of what, the poetic capacities of sociological facts can never be delimited. The harsh life of a coalminer
tells a story of the working class; events occurring in Australia in
a particular year tell the story of Australia; a survey involving
women tells what 'women' think; a description of an informant's
clothes is an analysis of the person; ethnographic description of
scenery or climate is like a sound effect or lighting change in the
theatre. Sociology often refuses to acknowledge these meta-narratives, but the discipline would be trivial without them and they
are embarrassing only in the context of a realism that denies its
own textuality and a literalism that denies its tropes (see
Atkinson 1990; Barthes 1986: 141ff; Carter 1988; Taussig 1989).

From literalism's viewpoint, meaning tends to the horror of
mess, escaping its proper place unless controlled through practices of linguistic hygiene and apartheid. Metaphor endangers
pure knowledge of the real. Once this fantasy is rejected, the creativity of the poetry of language can be appreciated and used
more effectively. An understanding of metaphoric play has profound implications for sociological practice, and the continuation
of this study will be a prolonged struggle with these implications.

* * *

To present men '*as acting*' and all things '*as in act*' – such could well be
the *ontological* function of metaphorical discourse, in which every
dormant potentiality of existence appears *as* blossoming forth, every
latent capacity for action *as* actualised.
   Lively expression is that which expresses existence as *alive*.
(Ricoeur 1986: 43)

Metaphor creates new meanings that enlarge the world and make
us dissatisfied with 'restorations' of the literal: the literal is not
our real meaning but a pallid rewriting of newly generated

metaphorical truths. Springing from our rapt attempt to understand the phenomena we confront, metaphor leaves us in a condition of wonder as the world newly understood is simultaneously made strange and elusive.

Etymologically, metaphor is associated with movement, metaphor being to language what migration is to social relations: through changing the relations of words in space, shifting words from their familiar neighbourhoods, it creates hybrid 'multicultural' meanings which are not predetermined and are always more than the sum of their parts. These new meanings can themselves be unsettled and resettled (see Deleuze and Guattari 1994: 96). The desire for literal meanings is akin to xenophobia's desire for an unchanging original oneness and imperialism's fear of differences it cannot colonise.

Chukovsky offers some lovely metaphors from very young children going about the everyday task of making meanings:

> 'Mommie, Mommie, the ship is taking a bath!'
> 'Mom, cover my hind leg!'
> 'Daddy, look how your pants are sulking!'
> 'Can't you see? I'm barefoot all over!' (1963: 1–3)

Because the meaning domains of words are never fixed, readers contend with metaphor's shocking juxtaposition of previously separate domains by imaginatively extending the domains' reach until the words find some common ground (see Turner 1991). An understanding of the ship taking a bath requires creation of a new class, into which both ships and bath-takers belong, and this reclassification unsettles ships and bath-takers. Readers will imagine this new class differently and may operate on feelings of meaning never consciously specified. Nevertheless I might make sense of the bathing ship by constructing a new class of 'water-loving bodies', in which both ships and bath-taking children belong. Once imagined, this class poses further questions (e.g. do ships have eyes and toes? do bath-taking children have rudders? is the bathtub an ocean, the ocean a tub?), unsettling and suspending my prior understandings of the limits of the meaning and nature of the world. Signs, therefore, are like people, existing within systems, deriving their meaning not from their internal nature but from relationships. Meaning comes from between and not just within.

Like dictionary definitions, classifications are codified metaphor, and when Chukovsky's children deterritorialise signs they un-self-consciously apply the logic of all classification systems. Cultural competence requires the improvisation of pathways of sameness through a limitless series of open and overlapping classification systems. Nothing belongs to one class alone. For example, while western science habitually associates cows and whales as mammals, popular culture may put whales and fish together as aquatic animals. Likewise, in certain contexts, hippopotamuses, ducks, ships and bath-taking children may belong together more than ducks and eagles do. Classifications are transformation systems, allowing the movement of meanings up, down and across the system's organised grid. Things are not simply themselves; with a simple shift of angle everything is something else, something more specific, more general, alike or contiguous in some way, its meaning located somewhere else. A human is a primate is a mammal; a human is Greek or the Greek is Socrates; a human is a lion or a sloth. A further metaphorical twist may generate a new system with axes of no previous salience.

The classificatory logic of metaphors also underlies many jokes of the 'topsy-turvy' type (Chukovsky 1963: 94ff). My son of 14 months laughed uproariously when I put a saucepan lid on my head, creating a metaphoric play between lid and hat. Children find delight in the rigorous nonsense of Mother Goose:

If all the world was apple pie
And all the sea was ink,
And all the trees were bread and cheese,
What would we have to drink?

These jokes, plays on meaning and words, highlight another crucial aspect of metaphor. The saucepan lid wouldn't have amused a child who didn't see it both as a hat and as not-a-hat. A statement about a growling boss likewise unsettles the verb 'to be' in the conventional assumption that 'the boss is human', convincing us that he is also something different, perhaps a lion. Keeping meaning suspended in play, metaphor insists that the boss both *is* and *is-not* a human, both *is* and *is-not* a lion. By maintaining an ironic tension between conventional sense and nonsense, and undermining literal notions of fixed and singular identity, metaphor transforms statements of being into processes of becoming. Without reaching resolution, these metaphoric statements of sameness and difference offer truths about how things actually are in the world they've re-created (Ricoeur 1986: 247–8).

Many people are disgusted and terrified by tolerance of the mess of this indeterminacy. 'Shame on you, Comrade Chukovsky,' wrote such a person,

> Children need socially useful information and not fantastic stories about white bears who cry cock-a-doodle-do. . . . We want [children's authors] to clarify for the child the world that surrounds him, instead of confusing his brain with all kinds of nonsense. (quoted in Chukovsky 1963: 89–90)

Whereas literal knowledge aspires to the inert status of information, metaphor works with indeterminacy to keep meaning safe from the final clarification that is its obituary. Meaning's play is not a game watched from the outside but one in which we live and through which we understand. We may fantasise about mastering literal knowledge, fixing it in our memories or reference books or filing cabinets, but metaphoric knowledges cannot be possessed, always maintaining reserves of wisdom beyond our present understanding. When someone criticised the lack of likeness in Picasso's portrait of Gertrude Stein, Picasso advised the person to wait. In the same way, the meaning of rich metaphors keeps blooming; people think further by growing into them, awakening to their implications. Traditions of thought grow stale with the declining productivity of their key metaphors.

According to Aristotle (1991: 215), good metaphors have a vividness that makes meaning lively. The child's metaphor of the ship taking a bath animates the inanimate, making us participate in meaning by imaginatively playing the role of the ship. By performing ship we lend our form to ship and thereby bring shipness to life for us. The saucepan lid lets the child play saucepan through his prior knowledge of hats. By having us act these roles, metaphor makes a world of ships and saucepans actual to us; our acting gives us an appreciation of how the world actually is.

Metaphoric actuality is not the same as the literal's reality, but we are sceptical of the literal's claim to re-present reality. Reality cannot really be seen, because we cannot see the world from the outside. Our knowledges are *ours*, mediated through us and projecting us into the world. We cannot fix or imitate the world as it really is, but we can create our own simulations of it through mime. As Benjamin noted, 'Perhaps there is none of [man's] higher functions in which his mimetic faculty does not play a decisive role' (1978: 333). By letting us live (in) the world, metaphors enliven our understandings. Weber was too modest when claiming that the faculty for compassion or empathy lets us understand other people: it underlies all metaphoric truth.

We do not come empty-handed to our performances of metaphor. When metaphor engages us, we respond through the emotions and memories that reverberate with the role. Our enactment of the world is a method acting informed and energised by the previous experiences that constitute us. We know ships because we remember the feeling of a bath; we know sulky pants by momentarily reliving our own moods; we know a growling boss because we have seen and imagined ourselves as lions. When performing a role, we are its stuff; we know it through lending it our form. Metaphor is a full-bodied and -emotioned way of knowing.

There is magic in metaphor's quicksilver ability to change the shape of the world and, like the sorcerer's apprentice, to call even inanimate objects to life. Instead of seeing the world mechanically, as a finitude of things connected by measurable forces, metaphoric knowledge understands it as the movement of creation, as 'potentialities of existence blossoming forth'. It blooms in this very text, this very moment.

* * *

In contemporary society rituals performed to stand-ins for supernatural entities are everywhere in decay, as are extensive ceremonial agendas involving long strings of obligatory rites. What remains are brief rituals one individual performs for and to another, attesting to civility and good will on the performer's part and to the recipient's possession of a small patrimony of sacredness. What remains, in brief, are interpersonal rituals. These little pieties are a mean version of what anthropologists would look for in their paradise. But they are worth examining. Only our secular view of society prevents us from appreciating the ubiquitousness and strategy of their location, and, in turn, their role in social organisation. (Goffman 1972: 89)

Other chapters argue that ritual is not only a basic sociological topic, but a basis of sociology, creating both a type of discipline and a form of knowledge. To underset this argument, however, I must redress a silence in conventional accounts of ritual: by highlighting ritual's reliance on metaphor, I wish to reclaim its relation to wonder and magic. All ritual trembles with sacred intimations of creation, as I will show by considering ritual as an everyday practice of metaphorical magic that allows us to act ourselves. Magic is used here with all its anthropological echoes, on the basis of a (metaphoric) interplay between the logic of tropes and magic's 'principles' of similarity and contagion (Frazer 1993: 11; see *Stories*). By celebrating metaphor's capacity to move us, the discussion will prepare for our account of a sociology that celebrates passionate knowledge.

I'll develop my analysis by taking a tiny example from the vast field of ritual, leaving you, as reader, to generate imaginatively a sense of the whole field. I will look at rituals of personal introduction common in my social circle, and specifically at the question of whether I would shake your hand if introducing myself to you in person.

In favourable circumstances, handshakes involve countless micro-responses which I apparently perform spontaneously, without will or decision. In other cases, my unease demands conscious attention and is overlaid with the worry that I seem anxious. I've been warned about wet-fish handshakes. A handshake implies levels of formality, equality and mutual recognition that require fine judgement and that operate on decisively different scales according to the sex, age and cultural background of the potential shakers. Perhaps a shake is inappropriate and a hug (how long? any back patting?), or a bow (how deep? standing how far apart? how many repeats?), or a nod, or smile, or a cheek kiss (one side? both sides? which side first? how many repeats?), or an air kiss, or a light mouth kiss, or a 'high-five', or a mumbled hands-in-pockets 'Hello' is the appropriate response. If the shake option is taken, further questions arise about who should initiate the shake, how long and hard to shake, whether to bring the second hand into a clasp over the shaking hands, whether to reveal your secret Masonic associations, or whether to display your allegiance to Lord Baden-Powell by shaking with your left hand.

Given handshaking's difficulties, it's wonder enough that we ever introduce ourselves, much less that these rituals usually work without any effort or concern. The same applies to the countless other micro-rituals by which we order our actions and interactions: queuing to enter a lecture theatre, passing salt at a dining table, selecting a bus seat, conducting small-talk, waiting in a lift, making or avoiding eye contact with strangers, choosing where to stand in a crowd. We negotiate the handshake, crowd or bus seat magically, without being aware how much is involved:

> I see you on the street; I smile, walk toward you, put out my hand to shake yours. And behold – without any command, stratagem, force, special tricks or tools, without any effort on my part to make you do so, you spontaneously turn toward me, return my smile, raise your hand toward mine. We shake hands – not by my pulling your hand up and down or your pulling mine but by spontaneous and perfect cooperative action. Normally we do not notice the subtlety and amazing complexity of this coordinated 'ritual' act . . . [unless] one has had to learn the ceremony only from a book of instructions, or . . . one is a foreigner from a nonhandshaking culture.
>
> Nor normally do we notice that the 'ritual' has 'life' in it, that we are 'present' to each other, at least to some minimal extent. As Confucius said, there are always the general and fundamental requirements of reciprocal good faith and respect. This mutual respect is not the same as a conscious feeling of mutual respect; when I am *aware* of a respect for you . . . our little 'ceremony' will reveal this in certain awkwardnesses. . . . Just as an aerial acrobat must, at least for the purposes at hand, possess (but not think about his) complete trust in his partner if the trick is to come off, so we who shake hands, though the stakes are less, must have (but not think about) respect and trust. (Fingarette 1972: 9)

Fingarette offers this analysis while developing Confucius' argument that magic and holiness are essential to human existence, that community is a holy rite. Acknowledging that most modern readers of Confucius are embarrassed by the 'quaintness' and 'impracticality' of these themes, Fingarette insists that

Confucius meant what he said, and that he was right – that 'truly, distinctively human powers have, characteristically, a magical quality' (1972: 6). Magic enlivens the most humble ceremonies, like handshaking introductions and saying 'please', a word children know as 'the magic word':

> It is important that we do not think of this effortlessness [of well-learned ceremonies] as 'mechanical' or 'automatic'. If it is so, then, as Confucius repeatedly indicates, the ceremony is dead, sterile, empty: there is no *spirit* in it. The true ceremony 'takes place'; there is a kind of spontaneity . . . Beautiful and effective ceremony requires the personal 'presence' to be fused with learned ceremonial skill. This ideal fusion is . . . [a] sacred rite. (Fingarette 1972: 8)

Confucius' belief in the sacredness of the secular resonates with Durkheim's theories of religion, ritual and sociality (1976). Ritual worked, Durkheim argued, by mobilising the energy people experience when assembled. Making people feel 'effervescent', it lifted their identities across previous boundaries, binding them emotionally to their neighbours as part of a bigger whole which functioned religiously even if it claimed secularity. Even ceremonies honouring individuals addressed 'the individualised forms of collective forces' (1976: 425). These arguments spill over the methodological quarantines that Durkheim himself set up to restrict sociology's dealings with 'psychological' states (see Durkheim 1964), and many critics chastise him for spoiling his case by relying on such emotional and bodily experiences as 'effervescence'. Durkheim's 'slip' is, however, a key opening for a passionate sociology.

In contrast to Fingarette and Durkheim, most popular and sociological accounts of contemporary western society tell of ritual's demise, of the enchanted woods withering under the scorching light of rationality, of witchcraft giving way to medicine, the mysteries to science, custom to bureaucracy and law. Ritual has come to mean empty, artificial and mechanical; its stuffy old fashions offend the cherished modern ideals of informality and individual autonomy, with their emphases on sincerity, immediacy and naturalness. Within these accounts, ritual is as suspect in action as rhetoric and figure in language. It is both prison and mask.

Fingarette's point, though, is that smoothly functioning ritual doesn't call attention to itself, and because it just happens, magically, as if its conventionality were a product of nature, it can be the medium for celebrations of immediacy. Indeed, from our sociological perspective, cultural forms like ritual and storytelling *are* our nature. Not only is nature culturally conceived, culture inhabits every aspect of our corporeality, from birth to death, with all the eating, sleeping, fornicating and excreting inbetween. It may be the vehicle for our lives, but it's not a prison for there's no outside.

Modern informality, for example, is itself generated through rituals that prescribe appropriate language, dress, body language and so on. Were these codes not present, how could people entering a setting adopt appropriately informal behaviour? How could actors produce 'informality' on stage? Directness and sincerity are also ritualised, requiring sustained eye contact, a certain tension (but not too much) in the body language, a certain ring in the voice. Without these codes, confidence tricksters and liars couldn't successfully perform sincerity.

Ritual is life's grammar, allowing us to improvise order in our actions over the time of their performance, to transform continually our sense of who we are and how we should act. Just as we must usually be unaware of our speech's grammar, graceful rituals cannot be performed self-consciously, for consciousness cannot organise so many micro-actions and -reactions. Responses are trained in our bodies and operate without call on consciousness. My right hand 'knows' it is the shaking hand; if I'm unexpectedly asked to identify my right or left, I impulsively mime a handshake and see which hand moves. In that moment my 'body' knows what my 'consciousness' does not. We're usually only conscious of problematic or anachronistic rituals.

When I offer my hand to someone, it moves through a complex sequence of tropic transformations that slide up and down the systems of classification (see Turner 1991: 147–8). This play leads people through the ritual's transformation. To illustrate the point, I'll imagine the sequence that might be involved in an effective handshake, bearing in mind that the actual sequence will depend on contextual factors. For this exercise I'll assume participants whose classification systems separate body and self.

The outstretched hand first harnesses a metonymic connection to signify the whole body. The hand is not the body, however, and this tension between is and is-not allows hands to negotiate the type of body they might signify: the body metonymically signified by the foot or face or genitals isn't the hand's body (a point highlighting the constructive quality of tropes). Because outstretched hands mark the body's outermost limit, they produce a public and formal, an outgoing, body.

The body signified by the hand itself operates as a metaphor for the self, so that the offered hand indirectly becomes a miming of my self, for me as well as my ritual partners. A hard hand (is a hard body) is a firm self; a sweaty hand is an insecure self; a length of the grasp may indicate the depth of the welcome; a refused hand is a rebuffed relationship. This accords with a familiar artistic convention that portrays hands in isolation as characterisations of a person. But just as hands signify a certain body, they signify a certain self. In western cultures, faces and hands are the two main public expressions of nakedness, and nakedness implies notions of true self. This implication is undermined, however, by other features of the hands. Hands are further than the face from the traditional seats of the self: they maintain a distance. Moreover, they are often seen as less direct and sincere because they come in pairs, evoking the possibility that they are 'two-faced' or 'two-tongued', that the person does not possess the oneness and sincerity expected of individuals. (People may try to insist on their sincerity by sealing the original handshake with their other hand.) A hand's body therefore signifies a public self that is open but not intimate or necessarily completely candid.

When two hands grasp in a handshake, the drama of metonymic contagion is enacted. Hands that celebrated separate selves suddenly become a bridge for mutual invasion. Recall the dramatic moment when Israeli and Palestinian leaders shook hands on the White House lawn: when two hands joined, two bodies, two selves, two peoples, touched. Without fences and quarantines, the two selves joined in a handshake flow into each other, and where there was once self and other, mutuality now creates an 'us'. In fraternal iconography, hands united have long signified people united. Nevertheless, the is-not is still not negated. The handshake allows contagion between self and other and honours the other by recognising him or her as a non-polluting source, but it is usually imagined as a controlled contagion.

My heartland self remains at a distance from the contact: I can tell myself that this is not an embrace, much less a sexual embrace involving bodily penetrations.

People who desire fixed and independent mastery are often so worried by handshaking's risk of contagion and mutuality that they protect themselves. Gloves offer the safety of condoms but nowadays speak too loudly of fear. If, however, I make my hand iron-hard, I am protected from mutuality. A soft, giving hand allows the other to rest against me, but an iron hand maximises my independence, leaving an impression on the other but allowing no return. I can only feel the other hand as a resistance that returns to me a feeling of my own power. I cannot even feel my own instrumental hand. This hardness may be strategic or may express a feeling unconsciously carried into the encounter; it may also be a hardness I neither intend nor feel but which is read into my handshake by my manual interlocutor. Such struggles for mastery usually destroy the grace and trust of Fingarette's handshakes, and the likelihood of such struggles often makes people uneasy about handshaking codes.

During those handshakes that involve mutuality, a magical transformation occurs. While the hands are joined, each hand, each body, each self, becomes a synecdochic signifier of 'us'. 'I' is now part of an 'us', a whole greater than the sum of its parts. If the selves of those shaking hands signify broader societies (e.g. nations, political movements, ethnic groups), the 'us' may be much larger than the two whose hands are joined. This is Durkheim's moment of effervescence, when people no longer recognise themselves, feeling in the grip or presence of some greater power. Because they actually become or perform this power, they feel a tangible living force rather than a lifeless abstraction. They know its actuality in themselves.

When a handshake has shaken its participants' selves, they leave it changed, knowing they've been metonymically touched or blessed by the greater force. This is a matter of degree, but even if the handshake only evokes feelings of civility or shared good manners, it involves some such change.

I have developed this analysis carefully because it shows how our most commonplace actions involve complex chains of metaphoric and magical transformation, nearly all working without our conscious control. Metaphor lives in us and we through it, its sinews as important to human action as the sinews of the anatomist. We want to awaken a wonder and respect for this everyday magic. The analysis also implicitly challenges sociology's orthodox assumptions about mind, body, self and world.

Bodies, this analysis suggests, are not a domain of nature covered in a thin cloth of culture; they are produced as cultural and social signifiers, sometimes consciously, most times not; they are written and performed, read and interpreted. Ritual metaphors move participants because the cultural codes are built into the body's ways. They animate us. My right hand acts out its cultural privilege over my left. In the ways I sit, clean my teeth, play the piano, walk, drive, write, touch myself, put myself to sleep: my body is not operating mechanically, it is performing 'me'. Different hands set up different border controls over different selves.

The 'me' performed in rituals like the handshake isn't stable, with a fixed script, but one that continually transforms to suit different situations and memories. Hamlet called for his 'too too solid flesh [to] melt', but this permanence is only one of flesh's countless forms, arising only when it performs solidity. Like Kafka's Gregor Samsa, in *Metamorphosis*, or Woody Allen's Zelig, or Arnold Schwarzenegger's rival in *Terminator II*, we magically change fleshy form to meet different situations: one moment I'm enacting an academic, then a university student, next I'm a cockroach scurrying to escape the heel of an important passer-by.

Because we're seldom self-conscious about rituals, we seldom assess their meaning consciously. We *feel* meanings, a term that indicates the intimate association between bodily senses and emotion. Like appropriately chosen grammar, a successful ritual feels right, comfortable, secure; it hums; perhaps we unconsciously nod our heads as we assure ourselves that everything's in order. We glide through such interactions as an effective handshake on a little cushion of well-being and satisfaction. Whereas Fingarette says a graceful ritual requires the other person's 'presence', such a test unnecessarily creates obsessional concerns that destroy the lightness of grace. Ritual only requires the feeling that the others are immediately present, and the unexamined space of trust between my feeling about the others and the others' feelings about themselves is precisely what allows the flow of civility and good manners. On the basis of faith, graceful ritual allows formal mutuality that doesn't descend into paranoid struggles for mastery.

An unsuccessful performance is likewise assessed intuitively: because it somehow feels wrong, it makes us anxious and disorientated and this precipitates conscious efforts to locate the problem in the spaces between selves and their ritual presentations. Am I uneasy, for example, because I've sensed some revealing inconsistency between the other's handshake and appearance? If I cannot solve the problem to my satisfaction, I usually continue the encounter self-consciously and mistrustfully, but this self-consciousness can immobilise me by removing my capacity to play myself. People with 'obsessional compulsive disorders', for example, may get physically stuck in doorways or wash their hands endlessly, unable to move on until they correct flawed performances (Rapoport 1991).

Although habit and custom are conventionally distinguished from ritual on the basis of a lack of awe, meaning and emotional commitment, such distinctions are difficult to sustain. If handshakes and passages through doors involve ritual work, what is left for habit? The small hum of awe may not be consciously recognised in small rituals of civility, experienced only as well-being or smooth sailing, but terrifying effects are unleashed if performances grind. Elias cites a wonderful case of an eleventh-century Greek princess who married a Venetian doge and insisted on maintaining the fork of the Byzantine table:

> This novelty was regarded as so excessive a sign of refinement that the dogaressa was severely rebuked by the ecclesiastics who called down divine wrath upon her. Shortly afterward she was afflicted by a repulsive illness and St Bonaventure did not hesitate to declare that this was a punishment of God. (1982: 68–9)

If the dogaressa's fork can become the devil's, and an illness become a message from God, it may be inappropriate to distinguish everyday rituals from larger scale performances.

Appreciation of ritual suggests that life isn't directly experienced as a singularity. Whereas identity implies self-sameness under differing conditions, life is conducted through fractured contexts, scraps of experience, differing levels of consciousness, transformations beyond the control of conscious decision, with no stable 'me' standing outside or behind the various presentations of self in particular situations. Moreover, self-representations inevitably bleed and contaminate: the most stringent semantic antisepsis can't stop essences ('vital bodily fluids') escaping, and invading, and mingling across the sacred boundaries of self. Other people's responses to my presentations must always be incorporated in my self-knowledges, just as my responses infiltrate their understandings of self. Being alone is not a primary pre-social condition, to which social life is added. It is only one type of social situation, and even in it I'm monitoring my performance and incorporating my assessments in my self-image.

So, whether we're talking about you, me, a nation or the discipline of sociology, a feeling of identity is a more or less fragile cultural achievement rather than a given. While I perform myself, I am not finally my own production, for much of the work occurs off-site and beyond my control or certain self-knowledge. I am a collective performance, an effect conjured in large part from the codes and clothes and smiles and handshakes and sanctions and training that constitute ritual. (Storytelling, another means of creating identity, is the topic of the next chapter.)

In one familiar pattern of usage, the term 'ritual' is specifically associated with magic, witchcraft, alchemy, conjuring and shamanism, but all ritual involves processes of non-mechanical transformation that could be described as magical. If ritual doesn't turn lead into gold, it either turns its participants from one sense of self to another or allows them to carry a self into a new social setting. All meaning is created through the play of metaphoric processes, and metaphor always has an element of magic about it.

Finally, if you're surprised that so much can be made of handshakes, consider the profound point this highlights: that all analyses are in principle endless. Analyses can always take a further step, make other links, move to other levels of specificity or abstraction. Through trope the smallest social incident can magically become part of some greater whole, just as the hand metamorphoses into the person or nation. Analyses end where they do because of pragmatic, aesthetic, conventional or topical considerations. When they imply that they're concluding because there is no more to say, they reveal more about literary and academic conventions than about the phenomena under investigation.

* * *

This chapter's role has been to destabilise conventional notions of objectivity, truth and identity, and replace them with understandings of the creative, full-bodied character of metaphor, ritual and cultural production more generally. In Porter's phrase, poetry is the guts of existence, and the distinctive qualities of a passionate sociology derive from its desire to proclaim rather than deny the discipline's passionate involvement in the world it studies. As other chapters show, this determination generates sociological practices and knowledges that run counter to many of the discipline's prevailing standards.

Stories

We are both storytellers. Lying on our backs, we look up at the night sky. This is where stories began, under the aegis of that multitude of stars which at night filch certitudes and sometimes return them as faith. Those who invented and then named the constellations were storytellers. Tracing an imaginary line between a cluster of stars gave them an image and an identity. The stars threaded on that line were like events threaded on a narrative. Imagining the constellations . . . changed . . . the way people read the night sky. (Berger 1984: 8)

In three volumes of stories, drawings, poems and essays, collectively entitled *Into Their Labours* (1985, 1989, 1991), John Berger has described the lives of contemporary European peasants. Having spent years living in a French peasant village, Berger presumably understands the villagers' lives as deeply as any ethnographer could, and his work displays the imaginative insight to which ethnographers aspire. Indeed an eminent anthropologist selected it as 'the finest summary of the nature of peasant society and its values and institutions' (Worsley 1984: 119). Nevertheless, despite its classical sociological subject matter, despite its basis in participant-observation, despite its deep understanding, implicitly drawn from engagements with social theory, the sociological credentials of *Into Their Labours* are unclear because overt storytelling is not one of the institutionalised modes within the discipline. There would be no such doubt, however, if the stories were reformulated as empiricist monologues: the narrator would withdraw from the text so that Truth or An Informant could speak directly, psychological shading would either be invented or eliminated entirely depending on the mode of causal explanation to be employed, traces of doubt and mystery (and honesty) would be hidden, more details would be specified, the language would be stripped of its overt poetry, tokens of methodological authenticity would be prominent, the incidents under consideration would be produced as a witness in a theoretical trial and would be superseded once this verdict was reached. And after all these changes were made in the name of sociological truth, the empiricist monologue would still be based on narrative fictions that denied their true character; it would remain a creation that refused to join with the reader in a celebration of dialogue and creativity.

Berger's achievement undermines the common sociological assumption that stories are aligned with fiction on the far side of truth. The difference between *Into Their Labours* and conventional academic studies is better seen in terms of genre and discipline than through distinctions between stories and studies, myths and truths, fact and fiction. While the facts of scientists and the fictions of novelists are created under significantly different disciplinary constraints, both try to simulate and tell truths about a world to which neither has unmediated access. As Williams argues, rigid distinctions between the two forms are a recent cultural production, based on 'a naive definition of the "real world", and then a naive separation of it from the observation and imagination of men' (1971: 41). Any assumption that explicitly realist accounts are more truthful than explicitly fictional ones is disconcerted by a comparison of parody, caricature and SF with realist writing and portraiture, which suggests that explicit falsity can often be the greater ally of truth and that truth always exists in the plural and at multiple levels.

Academic knowledge's commitment to truth is not belittled, then, by my claim that it necessarily relies on storytelling. Take, for example, the discipline of history, whose conventions weave through much sociological thought. As its name implies, this is a story-based discipline, but historians' stories are not ready-made and waiting in the world for report. Historians must create, select and order different facts from the limitless and never-completed stock; their stories are generated through their imaginative capacity to recognise how a selection of the facts can be organised around certain 'angles' into certain established narrative forms. However factual, these stories fabricate meaning fictionally, typically using the society's authorless sacred stories as their guides. Moreover, readers must recognise these myths, by their structures, in order to interpret the meaning or point of a history.

Marxist histories, for example, are only satisfyingly complete when readers feel the underlying presence of what may be called the Spartacus story, about the mortal combat between an oppressive master class and an inevitably rebellious slave class. This presence gives the family resemblance to Marxist histories, which are spatially and temporally specific variations on a timeless theme: 'The history of all hitherto existing society is the history of class struggle' (Marx and Engels 1971: 35).

History typically yearns for these formulas, which offer origin and order, but the task of historical reinterpretation is never completed, and a new generation cannot know itself unless it revises the historical foundation myth of its society. Historical debates, therefore, are based on historians cobbling stories around different mythic lasts. Their 'theories' are based on meta-narratives as beautiful and eternal as the sacred stories of allegedly pre-historical societies (see Lévi-Strauss 1978; White 1987).

While it might be possible to imagine other sociological forms, a pictorial or musical sociology for example, most sociology has also been a disciplined approach to writing stories. Based on historical accounts, informants' anecdotes, life histories, religious myths, fieldwork diaries; drawing on powerful theoretical meta-narratives about the evolution of humanity, the development of the state, the rise of capitalism, the changes in sexual relations, the spread of imperialism, the disenchantment of the world; using the formal conventions of biography, autobiography, gossip, myth, legend, thriller, fictional story, true story, horror story, romance, soap opera, traveller's tale; telling stories about nature, ourselves, the past and future, about neighbours, the cosmos, everyday chores – and stories: sociology's richness comes in part from the variety of ways it tells a variety of stories at a variety of levels. It comes also from the pleasurably disturbing way its stories open doors of possibility in the corridors of the everyday.

Sociologists who write in pleasing literary ways aren't the only sociological storytellers. Because of their need to create, select and arrange facts, and because their writing is held open by synecdoche, metonymy, metaphor and context, sociological writing cannot control its fictional or mythic capacities by exercising iron control over facts and signs. Texts always overflow their authors' intentions and facts. Just as the Bourgeois

Gentleman used prose without knowing it, most sociologists tell stories without knowing it (see Mulkay 1985).

* * *

> I am not . . . suggesting that man can or should sever himself from this [internalisation of historical narrative]. It is not in his power to do so and wisdom consists for him in seeing himself live it, while at the same time knowing (but in a different register) that what he lives so completely and intensely is a myth – which will appear as such to men of a future century, and perhaps to himself a few years hence, and will no longer appear at all to men of a future millennium. (Lévi-Strauss 1966: 255)

Because specialist workers should know the capacities of their tools, a sociologist conducting a survey is expected to consider research design, sampling and questionnaire design, the delivery and return of questionnaires and responses, the different ways of coding and statistically processing data. Non-specialists may feel these decisions are boring preliminaries to the real sociology, but because they actually generate the data to be analysed, they are a full part of the research results. Conclusions are produced and not found. Survey respondents are not pronouncing eternal verities; they are particular people answering particular questions on particular days, and sociologists can only make sense of these responses if they know what respondents were asked. This is why sociologists routinely discuss their 'methods' within the body of their texts.

These basic lessons are taught in methods courses in sociology departments around the world, but most sociologists don't apply them to the most important tools of their trade. For example, although sociology is proud of its studies of artistic convention and genre, it pays almost no heed to its own narrative conventions: sociologists tell stories as if they weren't storytellers, and as if storytelling were a less rigorous and honest pursuit than theirs. These topics are absent from almost all introductory sociology textbooks, despite the vast bulk of these tomes.

There is an inappropriate modesty in this refusal to discuss the technologies, conventions, disciplinary practices, labour processes and bodies through which social analysts experience and write about their world. Such issues are regarded as profane, in bad taste, wanky; sociologists should not be talking about themselves when more urgent external situations demand attention. This guilty fear of self-indulgence relates closely to Freud's critique of narcissism (1986), a 'complaint' which he said limited women's capacity to forgo self-centredness for universalistic notions of justice. With their selfless desire to serve the external love-object (the disadvantaged, the oppressed), sociologists have often presented themselves as the very model of the more advanced, civilised and masculine 'anaclitic' type whom Freud contrasts with the feminine narcissists. In terms of such a model, sociology has been formed around deeply masculine disciplines.

Far from making social analysis impossible or self-indulgent, an awareness of sociological artifice helps create positions from which sociologists can write stimulatingly and rigorously, positions that do not hide our own desires behind the subject positions that our knowledge creates, positions that allow a more ethical politics. When sociologists are masochistically or modestly silent about themselves, they deny their particularity and conventionality; they assume the voice of Modernity, Reason, Progress, Objectivity or the Universal, in all cases abstracted from specific corporeality, cultural form and institutional location. Sociology's diffidence about its labour process is like the screen that protected the power of the Wizard of Oz. There is, however, no intrinsic reason to maintain this practice of silence, for it is no more than the outcome of a disciplinary politics which remains in contention. It is possible to advocate and offer a more rigorous acknowledgement of the discipline's own practices, to insist that sociology's truths are not found but imaginatively fabricated with specific tools.

Some sociologists argue that little hinges on this debate. If all sociologists write stories, the only issue is whether to offer a token acknowledgement. Forms like the novel have no need to announce their creativity because they presuppose an imaginatively engaged reader. Sociology is not in this situation, however, for it has conventionally asked readers to keep their imaginations at the service of the literal. Accordingly, acknowledgements of creativity are a major issue in sociological ethics. Without them, the discipline claims a bullying power it cannot legitimate. With them, it is a more joyous, stimulating, passionate and democratic relation between sociologists and their readers. Sociology need not eschew such traditional forms as the empiricist monologue as long as the monologue tells of its telling, for this acknowledge-ment alone opens the monologue for re-writing by the reader.

Moreover, the acknowledgement has other consequences. All sociologists use stories, but narratives are not the only way of cre-ating meaning and reflexive sociologists are more likely to use a variety of writing forms to create new worlds and new possibili-ties for daily social practice. Poems, music, aphorisms, pictures, chronicles, meditations, essays, maps, structural analyses, lists, models, taxonomies, names, mathematical equations: these and other cultural forms may rely on unspoken stories, but even so they can organise experience in non-narrative ways, generating meanings inexpressible in the narrative form. In removing the explorers' and inhabitants' stories from the land, a map, for exam-ple, creates an abstract space that does not otherwise exist. Likewise, poems can express what stories repress. Because stories deal with life as a battlefield, with conflict, causality and resolu-tion, they tend to reduce moments and experiences to a place in a story. 'Poems,' on the other hand,

> regardless of any outcome, cross the battlefields, tending the wounded, listening to the wild monologues of the triumphant or the fearful. They bring a kind of peace. Not by anaesthesia or easy reas-surance, but by recognition and the promise that what has been experienced cannot disappear as if it had never been. . . . The promise is that language has acknowledged, has given shelter, to the experi-ence which demanded, which cried out. (Berger 1984: 21)

Because of these differences, a reflexive sociologist might find poetry better adapted than narrative to capture moments as moments, experiences as experiences.

For many analysts, Brecht's development of the epic as an alternative to Aristotelian drama exemplifies the search for the (literary) forms best suited to the task at hand. The Aristotelian form commonly found in stories is so comfortable that even when its 'content' is troubling, its promise of cathartic resolution offers the deep nostalgia of homecoming. Brecht gained other theatrical possibilities by 'showing showing', giving little shocks to push the emotions from their homing pigeon path. Characterising it as a seismology rather than a semiology, Barthes has described the method eloquently:

> All that we read and hear covers us like a layer, surrounds and envelops us like a medium: the logosphere. This logosphere is given to us by our period, our class, our metier: it is a 'datum' of our subject. Now, to displace what is given can only be the result of a shock: we must shake up the balanced mass of words, pierce the layer, disturb the linked order of the sentences, break the structures of the language.... Brecht's work seeks to elaborate a shock-practice ...; his critical art is one which opens a crisis: which lacerates, which crackles the smooth surface, which fissures the crust of languages, loosens and dissolves the stickiness of the logosphere; it is an *epic* art: one which discontinues the textures of words, distances representation without annulling it. (1986: 213)

Sociologists who recognise their storytelling are more likely to understand that narratives limit the production of meaning even as they enable it. This recognition is not an admission of failure but a more accurate, full and open account. Rather than vainly denying the living power of stories, such sociologists are putting stories in their place.

* * *

> Ooey Gooey was a worm. Ooey Gooey went for a stroll on a railroad track. Along came a railroad train.
>
>   Ooey gooey!
> (... the simplest known instance of the temporising of essence ...)
>   (Burke 1961: 257)

To be comprehensible, stories must use recognisable conventions of form, one of which is the obvious feature of sequentiality. By highlighting this single example, we will see more clearly how narrative form shapes the truths that sociological stories can tell.

Stories connect events in time. In Forster's formulation, their basic structure is 'And then.... And then.... And then....' (1962: 44–5). As this implies, stories usually conceive of time lineally, as a long, irreversible, evenly-spaced sequence in which earlier events come first and cause later ones. Unless there are contrary indications, most stories also imply that the passage of story time directly mirrors the passage of time being 'described'. Just as the minutes of clock time pass in fixed sequence, the story passes word by word and perhaps page by page, from beginning to end.

Aristotle focused on narrative sequence when he characterised drama as the arrangement of incidents into a plot with beginning, middle and end (1987: 546). Rather than endearingly obvious, this is an unsettling observation. Lévi-Strauss made a similar point in different terms:

> like articulate speech, but unlike painting – [myth and music require] a temporal dimension in which to unfold. But this relation to time is of a rather special nature; it is as if music and mythology needed time only in order to deny it. Both, indeed, are instruments for the obliteration of time. Below the level of sounds and rhythms, music acts upon a primitive terrain, which is the physiological time of the listener; this time is irreversible and therefore irredeemably diachronic, yet music transmutes the segment devoted to listening to it into a synchronic totality, enclosed within itself. Because of the internal organisation of the musical work, the act of listening to it immobilises passing time; it catches and enfolds it as one catches and enfolds a cloth flapping in the wind. It follows that by listening to music, and while we are listening to it, we enter into a kind of immortality. (1986: 15–16; see also Crites 1989)

Music with a beginning and an ending *is* a piece and is not just *of* a piece. Anyone familiar with western music understands the formal conventions which indicate musical closure: a tension strains a coda until the music resolves by returning to the original key of the piece. It has rounded itself off. These phrases emphasise that the ending is a return to its beginning, involving the re-establishment of an emotional balance lost in the middle of the piece. Unlike the musical fragment snatched when switching radio stations, a piece of music denies the time between beginning and ending. The historical genres of annal and chronicle relate to the historical narrative as the scrap of music relates to the piece. Although their readers may hunger to narrativise them, the annal lacks both beginning and ending while the chronicle doesn't so much conclude as cut off. Neither form resolves itself.

Beginnings and endings usually pretend to reflect the passage of time in a pre-cultural reality, as evident in the glorious phrase 'To begin at the beginning', with which Dylan Thomas begins

Under Milk Wood. Notwithstanding the implication that the play takes its opening from a real beginning, Captain Cat, Polly Garter and the others only exist in Thomas's text, in the time suspended between the tick of its beginning and the tock of its ending. The claim of a real beginning time and place is a poetic attempt to create verisimilitude. When not narrativised, life may not have beginnings, which Aristotle defines as 'that which is not necessarily the consequent of something else, but has some state or happening naturally consequent on it' (1987: 546). Nor need non-narrativised life have Aristotelian endings, 'a state that is the necessary or usual consequent of something else, but has itself no such consequent' (1987: 546). Beginnings and endings are cultural creations, the start and conclusion of stories. They are connected teleologically so that the beginning inevitably implies an end that returns to the beginning. In stories, events 'unfold' as manifested destiny, and a story that fails to return is likely to be received as a failed story, pointless or unsatisfactory.

Another implication of the relation between beginnings and endings is that the meaning of the beginning must be deferred until the ending. Events which we consider beginnings later appear as continuations, as many of us sadly observe when we inspect the tatters of our worthy New Year's resolutions. Think, on the other hand, of the crisis generated when someone suddenly tells their spouse that they want a divorce. The beginning of this story can only be seen in retrospect; when it was occurring people were unaware of its full significance. Beginnings are always written from hindsight: they are stories created later, from the perspective of what we have become, through which we constitute our sense of what we are. Not only can we never again be or fully know what we were at any beginning, we couldn't then know either *if* something were beginning or *what* was beginning. If the past is another country, it is colonised through stories. This continual need to rewrite the past in the context of the present, to populate it with the precursors of later issues, is one of the reasons crises disorientate people, making them feel cheated. They *have* been cheated – of the past as it was experienced.

Most sociological storytellers naively believe they can begin their studies at some natural beginning and end at some natural ending, and that in doing so they will celebrate time, change and history. Paradoxically, like Lévi-Strauss's myths and music, sociological stories usually negate the time and creativity they seek to celebrate, for their beginnings and endings exist simultaneously, each inevitably implying the other, each trimmed for the task of holding the middle. In a story, 'a man who dies at the age of thirty-five is at every point of his life a man who dies at the age of thirty-five' (quoted in Benjamin 1970: 100), but this isn't the perspective through which he and others lived those thirty-five years. Sociologists who use narrative carelessly are distorting his life by brutally rejecting the specificity of the experiences that constituted it.

In a little-known book entitled *The Beginning Was the End*, Oscar Kiss Maerth (1974) earnestly argues that humans bear as an unchangeable essence the marks of their evolutionary genesis: as cannibal apes that acquired intelligence through eating brains. Sadly, or not, Maerth hasn't discovered the secret of humanity and human evolution; his title simply describes the narrative form he uses! Many better-known social analysts also make this mistake. The perfect fit and closure they enjoy at the end of their historical explanations of modernity, capitalism and nationalism is not the beauty of Truth but narrative's circularity. They have *assumed* the narrativity of history.

* * *

> every writer *creates* his own precursors. His work modifies our conception of the past, as it will modify the future. (Borges, quoted in Foucault 1977b: 5)

Although sociology doesn't pre-exist the diverse labours of sociologists, and although it imaginatively generates the objects it studies (e.g. society, culture, nations, imperialism, genders, classes), most sociology textbooks unblushingly define the discipline as if it were a fixed and external object, identifying its essence as surely as Maerth locates human nature. Like Maerth, the textbooks base their essentialism on an unacknowledged narrativity, relying on storytelling to make their accounts reassuringly certain and to give sociology a coherence and historical trajectory.

This narrativity can be shown by returning to the textbooks' honour rolls of 'founding fathers'. These rolls aren't simply lists, for they are rarely arranged arbitrarily, by alphabet or year of the father's birth: they are fictional plots, without an acknowledged author. While apparently discussing this writer and then this, the textbooks are implicitly describing sociology's genesis and development, as if sociology were a thing capable of progress, as if that progress culminated in the textbook. The litany constitutes an origin myth, celebrating not what sociology was but what the textbook now says it is. Within this myth, the fathers are reduced to bearing sociology's destiny by redressing their predecessors' misconceptions or lacunae. Ideas falling outside the present conception of progress are discreetly erased or trivialised.

The textbooks' unacknowledged narrativity leaves its trace in tensions marking every honour roll. Almost without exception, founding fathers are white men from the United States or the imperial powers of Western Europe, and yet most textbooks define sociology as the intellectual pursuit of a universal natural object called 'society'. This imbalance isn't addressed by the textbooks, leading to the implication that it reflects the more advanced intellectual condition of the western metropolitan societies. Other societies must import their sociological self-knowledge along with their capital, cars and computers. The universal definition of sociology also sits uneasily with the textbook stories of how the founding fathers were preoccupied by specifically western experiences like the French and Industrial Revolutions, dealing with them in historically specific terms like feudalism, capitalism, socialism, the family, the state, economics, art, religion, culture and society. The textbook stories repress these tensions, but the uneasiness they cause is evident in textbook sociology's guilty boundaries with anthropology and history. If sociology studies society, why has it ceded most societies to anthropologists and historians? These disciplines are its supplements, tidying up the imperial differences it denies but can't eliminate.

The variations between the honour rolls of a French (Aron 1965), an American (Coser 1971) and a British textbook (Raison 1979) undermine even the notion of a single western sociology. Four of Coser's twelve *Masters of Sociological Thought* are American, but none appear on Aron's list in *Main Currents in Sociological Thought*, which includes four Frenchmen in its seven fathers; ten of Raison's thirty-one *Founding Fathers of Social Science*

are British but none reaches Aron's list and only one reaches
Coser's. The textbooks promise sociology in the singular but give
national stories.

The implicit textbook stories are also unclear about whether
the founding fathers are sociologists or writers in whom sociologists recognise their own concerns. On the one hand, most lists
include Comte because he coined the term 'sociology', even
though few sociologists now read his work. On the other hand,
the lists include many fathers who either predated sociology or
rejected this appellation. The former category includes Plato,
Aristotle, Ibn Khaldun, Montesquieu, Rousseau, Saint-Simon; the
latter includes de Tocqueville, Mill, Mead, Gramsci, Adorno,
Malinowski, Radcliffe-Brown and, most embarrassingly, Marx. If
many 'founders' of sociology weren't sociologists (or social scientists) and didn't see 'society' as their object of study, the lists'
rationale collapses, along with sociology's secure boundaries, for
every sociologist has a radically different list of major influences
who can be recruited to the honour roll. Sociology's genesis
occurs continuously, Vico (1668–1744) recently emerging as a
founding father and Montesquieu belatedly included as the first
father in the second edition of Raison's book. Each new origin
changes the imagination of current sociology and allows yet more
origins.

I don't deny the value or pleasure of intellectual family trees,
for my own ideas often arise from connections 'found' between
the work of different writers. My created lineages, however, are
read both up and down – I must originate my origins. Intellectual
family trees chart not the imperturbable logic of causality but the
imaginative logic of storytelling. I imaginatively create the 'struc-
turalists' who develop out of 'structural-functionalism' and my
'Marx', 'Weber' and 'Durkheim' are generated from my particular readings. Familial storytelling opens up new questions, but it
only playfully defers the discontinuities, accidents, coincidences,
contradictions and deviations that unsettle any account.

The honour roll stories betray a desire to systematise sociology
around an essence or classical 'core', but the tensions in sociology's self-presentation ensure it remains a *nervous* system, a state
of emergency its normal state of being (Taussig 1992).
Institutional knowledges are called disciplines for good reason,
the urbane tolerance at the centre of sociology being matched by

sometimes brutal activities in its border regions, where guards patrol in the name of the founding fathers, protecting the discipline's 'integrity' from the incursions, profanations and seductions of improper sociology. Storytellers who proclaim themselves the legitimate children of founding fathers insult and colonise the books, authors and past they claim to honour, reducing them to testing grounds for their own concerns. If Marx had to disown Marxism because he couldn't recognise himself in his acolytes' claims, pity the dead writers who can't disown their 'children'.

Stories of sociology's founding fathers are origin myths generating solidarities and terrors. They are as circular and essentialist, as covertly creative, and as reliant on representational fantasies as the definitions found beside them in textbooks. They rely on forgetting the effects of their narrative form.

* * *

People . . . awaken to a sacred story, and their most significant mundane stories are told in the effort, never fully successful, to articulate it. For the sacred story does not transpire within a conscious world. It forms the very consciousness that projects a total world horizon, and therefore informs the intentions by which actions are projected into that world. . . . One may attempt to name a sacred story . . . [but] such naming misleads as much as it illuminates, since its meaning is contained – and concealed – in the unutterable cadences and revelations of the story itself. (Crites 1989: 71)

So, in the beginning is a story: perhaps the story of the universe's Big Bang, or the story of the deluge brought by the great Snake Yurlunggur; perhaps the story of the first human using the first tool, or the story of how sons killed, consumed and then worshipped their father; perhaps the story of the rise of industrial capitalism, or the story of how nineteenth-century social analysts like Marx, Weber and Durkheim founded the discipline of sociology. Many writers have characterised narrative as one of the great transcultural transhistorical universals of human culture – 'Not, in origin, an artefact of culture, an art, but a fundamental operation of the normal mind functioning in society. To learn to speak is to learn to tell a story' (Le Guin 1989: 39). Such universalisms are common founding moments in social analysis, based on stories about human nature and development, but *homo sapiens, homo faber, homo loquens, homo bellicosus, homo ludens* and the rest normally fail at the first test, unable to account for their own narrativity. Because beginnings are always the start of stories, narrative's own claim to a privileged position has a beautiful logic that cannot be so easily dismissed. I will argue, moreover, that narrative's role puts issues of morality and religion at the centre of subjectivity, sociality and sociology.

By showing storytelling at work in unconscious and non-verbal experience, dreams neatly demonstrate its fundamental character (see Le Guin 1989: 39–40). If awakened during the rapid eye-movement stage of sleep, people report dreams as jumbled fragments of imagery; awaken them during quiet sleep, and their dreams take a 'proper' narrative form, embedding the bizarre shards of image into a comprehensible narrative form. Even when asleep, without artistic intent, we use stories to organise the chaos of our experience. Experience does not come naturally packaged in stories; we work with memory and anticipation to create a narrative that renders the world comprehensible and therefore liveable. Narrative ceaselessly changes the meaning of experience.

This applies outside dreams, of course. The neurologist Oliver Sacks tells the story of his patient William Thompson, whose memory span had been reduced to a few seconds. Mr Thompson could not, for example, remember the doctors who came to see him, but on the basis of the jumbled evidence before him (their dress, age, tone of voice, etc.), he instantly created stories about who his visitors were, why they were there and how he should, accordingly, act. When the doctors denied being mechanics or delicatessen customers, he would unflinchingly enter a new story by recombining the evidence at hand:

> He was continually disoriented. Abysses of amnesia continually opened beneath him, but he would bridge them, nimbly, by fluent confabulations and fictions of all kinds. For him they were not fictions, but how he saw, or interpreted, the world. Its radical flux and incoherence could not be tolerated, acknowledged, for an instant – there was, instead, this strange, delirious, quasi-coherence, as Mr Thompson, with his ceaseless, unconscious, quick-fire inventions

continually improvised a world around him – an Arabian Nights world, a phantasmagoria, a dream of ever-changing people, figures, situations. (1986: 104)

As subjects, we are not bodies, minds or emotions; it is our stories about such things that generate our sense of being uniquely ourselves through time as well as space. We do not just tell stories, we live them; they do not simply describe reality, they constitute it, not as a God might, from outside, but as part of reality's very stuff. Like the words 'history', '*Geschichte*' and '*histoire*', the terms 'life' and 'biography' are deeply ambiguous, referring to both the narration of and existence within a passage of time. Mr Thompson's confabulations were a desperate attempt to save his life, in this double sense. Because he was terrified by amnesia's theft of his biography, he fabricated himself every few seconds.

What distinguishes Mr Thompson is his memory, not his storytelling; we all ceaselessly tell stories, which we live out, which constitute us, our present and future. Stories also constitute our past, though the stories of our present may be completely revised before being submitted to memory and becoming our past. Not only do stories normally structure human memory, ensuring that the jumble of experience is later re-presented as if it had naturally come to us in narrative form, but memories not structured this way, taking perhaps the form of typologies or lists, are harder for the human memory to hold. In Mr Thompson's case, however, the storytelling functions spun wildly, finding no purchase in a memory that no longer allowed him to build coherent patterns into his life.

Each of these life stories promises some kind of moral or point. Stories are not simply given, as objects; they are sets of active relations between the author and text and the text and audience, and the words do not constitute a story if the reader doesn't get 'the point'. This is not to say that the reader must find the moral intended by the author, but without a point a story might be more accurately termed a chronicle or annal. In telling Mr Thompson's story, for example, my point has been to suggest that stories are fundamental to the processes of identity- and meaning-creation. After creating what it is to be human, Australian, a sociologist or a unique named individual, stories

construct us as humans, Australians, William Thompson or whatever. I am *suggesting* this point because I cannot exhaustively test
every meaning and identity; I can only tell persuasive exemplary
stories about stories. We approach knowledge crabwise, avoiding
direct answers. 'Mummy, where did I come from?' 'Doctor, why
am I dying?' Even basic questions cannot be answered directly;
first we sit down and tell stories, about social relations, the workings of the body or the will of God. Two sociologists in discussion
may appear to give each other direct and non-narrative answers,
but only because unspoken stories dwell in their specialist jargon
about capitalism, patriarchy and so on.

Stories are generally told about the exceptional because the
normal or canonical is normally invisible. A story about the normal would have no point, unless its perversity (i.e. exceptionality)
made readers think it was, precisely, a story *about* nothing.
Nevertheless, stories apparently about the exceptional also
address the normal, by implicitly producing normality as part of
the opposition that defines the exceptional. Moreover, in fully
characterised stories these oppositions become unstable as the
audience comes to realise that the exceptional is not, after all, so
remarkable. This instability is well expressed in the common
story opening of 'One day . . .', which holds out promises of both
ordinary and extraordinary days. By telling William Thompson's
exceptional story, Sacks shows how identity *normally* works; he
invites us to consider the remarkable quality of normal biogra-
phies. This pleasurable shock of recognition is his deeper point.
Stories take us 'into the woods', to the edges of our ordinary
lives, where anything can happen, where all possibilities can be
imagined, where we might live but for chance, choice or fate. In
doing so, stories test our selfhood and make us re-create ourselves. Those who join Mr Thompson at the abyss where
biography disappears are extended the opportunity to re-evalu-
ate the creative role of storytelling in their lives. So while stories
are, at one level, about the exceptional, at another they are about
the ordinary, and at a third about links between the ordinary and
exceptional.

It follows that stories always focus on the limits of normality
and legitimacy. A common story form relies on Trouble entering
a setting and disturbing the previous balance between actors,
goals, objects and so on (see Bruner 1990: 50). Whether it's the

arrival of the Cat in the Hat, or of the poverty that leads to the
abandonment of Hansel and Gretel, Trouble requires moral decisions of characters and hypothetical decisions of listeners and
readers. Despite earnests of dispassionate objectivity, even the
stories of science are evaluative: Who tells cancer's side of the
story? Why is economic inflation a virus? The moral character
of stories is conveyed when children 'tell tales' on one another. It
is also in gossip's bad name: judgement and policing are necessarily involved in the stories that allow community members to
monitor one another's activities and rework their story of collective identity.

When conscious of our storytelling, we are usually telling
stories about stories, clarifying, elaborating or reminding ourselves of the deeper 'sacred' stories about who we are, why
we're here, how the world works. The deepest stories, though,
are beyond direct telling, less monuments to be admired than
dwelling places that give our lives form and shelter (Crites 1989:
70). It is difficult to know if we tell our sacred stories or they tell
us. Thus Lévi-Strauss's classic studies of myth claim to show
'not how men think in myths, but how myths operate in men's
minds without their being aware of the fact' (1986: 12). But precisely because we live through them, carrying them around in
our bodies, these stories cannot be directly or fully told from an
external perspective. Certainly sociology offers no external van-
tage, with Lévi-Strauss admitting that his study is itself
mythological and that he finally cannot say if the thought
processes of South American Indians find expression through
his intellectual work or whether his thought processes find
expression through theirs (1986: 12–13). Yet if we cannot directly
tell our deepest stories, we know they exist because we recognise them when they resonate with the more ordinary stories
that can be told. Even a cheap murder mystery or love story
may move us because of its faint echoes of stories about the
meaning of life and love. In the best sociological stories, the
echoes can be almost palpable.

The real treasure from my sociological research projects has
been the anecdotes that have made themselves at home in my
imagination, resonating with intimations of the sacred that I can
feel but not tell, demanding that I come to terms with their beauty
and strangeness. My analytical writing turns these anecdotes

around and around, like river pebbles in my palm, testing different ways of telling them, but while these various tellings are more or less satisfying, and more or less useful for identifying subsidiary issues, they never exhaust the enigma of the 'originals'. The best stories have a 'chaste compactness' that both encourages and defies analysis (Benjamin 1970: 91).

I often return my sociological stories to the people who inspired them, but as a gesture of reciprocity more than a test of my account's truth. Stories are bountiful, and a story's use by one person does not lessen its availability to those who may find different truths. Stories are stray cats, giving a home as they make one on your lap, but remaining no one's possession. Not right or wrong, current or discarded, stories are 'the seeds of grain which have lain for centuries in the chambers of the pyramids shut up air tight and have retained their germinative power to this day' (Benjamin 1970: 90).

* * *

As the act of the poet is met – and it is the full tenor and rites of this meeting which I would explore – as it enters the precincts . . . of our being, it brings with it a radical calling towards change. The waking, the enrichment, the complication, the darkening, the unsettling of sensibility and understanding which follow on our experience of art are incipient with action. Form is the root of performance. In a wholly fundamental, pragmatic sense, the poem, the statue, the sonata are not so much read, viewed or heard as they are *lived*. The encounter with the aesthetic is, together with certain modes of religious and of metaphysical experience, the most 'ingressive', transformative summons available to human experiencing. (Steiner 1989: 143)

Why is there magic in the phrase 'Once upon a time'? Why is storytelling so deeply comforting, even when we are attending to horror stories? Why are we drawn by our hunger for beginnings and endings?

Shall I tell a story in answer? What else could I do?

The easy response to these questions invokes a 'natural' curiosity about origins and the past, but this response is undermined by the argument that beginnings are of and about the present. More plausible is Said's claim that beginnings (and endings) reveal an imaginative and emotional desire for order and unity, 'a need to apprehend an otherwise dispersed number of circumstances and to put them in some sort of telling order, sequential, moral, or logical' (1978: 41). This is a created and not a found order. To create and order ourselves we tell metaphysical stories about how we came to be as we are; by refusing to acknowledge the power of narrative form we pretend that our existence and order are fixed, external, secure, that there are boundaries, that there are reasons. Bedtime stories comfort children with promised lands where things begin, where lost order, restored, reigns 'ever after'. When Ludwig Bemelmans (1992) ends the children's book *Madeline* with the lovely bedtime lines:

'Good night, little girls!
Thank the lord you are well!
And now go to sleep!'
said Miss Clavel.
And she turned out the light —
and closed the door —
and that's all there is —
there isn't any more.

he offers a perfect snuggly security by imagining order and knowledge as a book whose final page or a room whose door can be closed. The world is finite and ordered; everything has a proper place; history ends and trouble leaves forever when order is restored. The lord knows, the angels look down.

Even when we reorder our self-conceptions, through crises, our new stories pitch the original moment into the past and claim simply to have unearthed and re-presented it. This denial involves a defensive and legitimatory logic, reframing politico-cultural history and creative historiography as natural history and empirical historiography. Our concepts of our nature, essence or identity act as 'character' does in Aristotle's theory of tragedy, bringing about 'change' but as an unfolding as inevitable as Ooey Gooey's sticky end.

We do not, however, simply *tell* stories, we retell them. It is not enough to read 'Little Red Riding Hood' to the child once; we regularly flick through our photograph albums in search of the familiar stories; we have yearly anniversaries in commemoration of birth, wedding and other stories; we watch the same TV show every Tuesday night; the annual Christmas dinner is based on the same stories, the same people, the same food. This ritualised repetition of stories structures our lives and reaffirms the promise of order, but its compulsive quality suggests that the promise is never fulfilled, that narrative order is unstable. Strictly speaking, we can never even *repeat* our stories, because every telling changes us and them. In retelling stories, therefore, we re-create rather than recapture our selves, and we do so because 'ever after' only exists in stories. This is Sondheim's point in *Into the Woods* when Cinderella destabilises the 'happy ever after' of his penultimate line by blurting out a final wish, repeating the desires which brought the trouble in the first place. We repeat the narrative promises ever after to revive their effects, because we cannot actually live ever after, happily or not.

A compulsion to return to origins is not only well documented in anthropological accounts of myth, it may be why anthropology is fascinated by myth and why western society is fascinated by anthropological accounts of 'the primitive'. Eliade, for example, argues that ritual in 'traditional' societies returns people to the time of Creation, allowing ritual performers to reanimate the present with the energy of genesis. This process of 'eternal return' exhibits a circular logic: 'the man of a traditional culture sees himself as real only to the extent that he ceases to be himself (for a modern observer) and is satisfied with imitating and repeating the gestures of another' (Eliade 1954: 34). Such conservatism should not, however, be taken at face value. The qualities 'conserved' are themselves created; the ritual engendering this creativity refers to the past, but the past of the present. In this sense, the ritual performers are not deluded to feel the grip of the creative moment, for in re-creating the past they give birth to the present. Within cosmogonies, the original is still originary, conservatism is creative.

The point holds for sociological narratives. It is understandable that readers respond to stories of epoch-making social processes with awe as well as comfort, for they are indeed witnessing a great and world-making event, the genesis of a new past and consequently a new present. The original creative spark *is* animating the present, 'reminding' readers of self-definitions they might never have previously known.

Narrative, this implies, is connected with the sacred. Stories are ritual activities or performances, their narrativity only emerging in the spellbound communion between audience and teller. These performances obey special ritual codes which separate them from the profane world where other rules apply and where the dirt of disorder threatens. One such code is a conventionalised beginning, which ushers listeners through a portal and into the story, removing the soiled garb of their daily life and preparing them for the mystery and enchantment of 'once upon a time'. Throughout the story other ritual gestures will affirm the social relations involved in narrative performance, ensuring that the audience stays 'with' the teller. The oral storyteller will use eye contact, rhythm, direct address, body language and vocal inflections to engage listeners, and literary storytellers have analogous techniques, some of which are discussed in *Ink*. Through these ritual practices they maintain the emotional communion that gives them the authority to lead their audience further on, towards the close of the ceremony.

The storyteller is like a priest or magician, a specialist guide through the separate and protected world of the sacred. As Lévi-Strauss noted, story time offers cosmogonic whispers of immortality, a no-time, an all-time, a liminal space within the flow of mundane life. 'Neither here nor there', it is 'betwixt and between' the social positions set out for the conduct of ordinary life (Turner 1969: 81). Stories are a space and time of passage where people can change themselves by returning to beginnings: 'the Nay to all positive structural assertions, but . . . in some sense the source of them all, and, more than that, . . . a pure realm of possibility whence novel configurations of ideas and relations may arise' (Turner 1970: 97).

If storytelling is a sacred world-forming performance, what of sociological storytelling? This question can be explored through an example, charged with the usual measure of metonymic and synecdochic play (based on Taussig 1992: 149ff). Imagine I had the task of analysing a Christian funeral service. At one level the service deals with death's disorder, helping the bereaved come to terms with mortality. Occurring at a time of great sorrow and doubt, the ceremony moves the bereaved by having them relive the deceased's life as this story is celebrated in obituaries, anecdotes, favourite music, photographs and so on. This narrative movement of emotion prepares the bereaved to accept a shift in the life's meaning: while it still pulses in the congregation, the priest inserts the deceased's life into a broader story, making sense of death's arbitrariness and finality by connecting them with God's purpose and promise, present in the rituals involving Bibles, crucifixes, hymns and other sacred artefacts. The service comforts the congregation by responding to the existential questions raised by death.

At a second interpretative level, however, I might suggest that the ceremony is 'really' about the 'bigger' issue of social structure, and that its efficacy derives from its ability to heal the social body by leading the congregation through a dramatic catharsis. On this view, the deceased's body represents the horror of the social body wounded when death disrupts networks and relationships. The ceremony reunites the dislocated group, affirming that society survives the death of particular members, and the active bonds linking people as the singing and sobbing congregation are experienced as the tangible proof of the presence of this greater unity and purpose. Although my analysis presents the first 'religious' story as raw evidence and the second as subsequent sociological interpretation, the second is built into the first, which was described specially so it could serve the second. Most sociologists would also refuse to acknowledge that the 'sociological' level is itself a narrative performance, like the priest's. Just as the priest temporarily revives the deceased's life, I tell a story to bring the ceremony (back) to life in readers' imaginations so that I can then inscribe it in the broader sociological context, using evidence of collective action to prove society's presence at the rite.

If my interpretation of the funeral service doesn't acknowledge its own storytelling, it generates a third narrative level, naturalising the notion of social structure so that it becomes 'the rock-hard referent of the real' rather than a sociological production (Taussig 1992: 151–2). While reading my story about the magical effects of an Aristotelian narrative catharsis, readers are encouraged to undergo their own narrative journey, venturing through exotic religious customs, unsure of whether sociological knowledge will be vindicated. The more they read the deterritorialised sociological account of grieving spouses, mourning clothes, hearses, hymns, candles, vestments and prayers, the thicker their uncertainties, the greater their desire for a recapture of sociological control. A final sociological redemption of order offers readers a catharsis of their own, encouraging emotional and intellectual acquiescence to the claim that social structure 'really' exists. My account is performed in the manner of a shaman or priest, and sociology's theoretical order is the third patient, healed through work on its surrogates, the corpse and the body of the congregation. This is the hidden magic operating whenever case studies refuse to acknowledge their narrativity. They promise the security of a fixed knowledge on which the door can be closed.

Sociologists, anthropologists, priests and shamans all operate by creating other worlds in narrative form, making one world plausible by relating it to another, slipping between registers, slipping from parts (obituaries, the congregation) to wholes (lives, human society) and back again. All operate, in other words, through the human faculty for mimesis or miming (see Auerbach 1968; Taussig 1993). Where the priest has the Bible and the obituary, the sociologist has names, examples, case studies, photographs, maps, stories, tables, interview responses, all of which use the magical processes of similarity and contagion, and the related figurative processes of metaphor, metonymy and synecdoche, to acquire the power of the things they're meant to represent. Whereas the priest reifies and fetishises the sacred, the sociologist reifies and fetishises 'society', 'social structure' and 'the real'. The law of similarity binds most sociological texts and their 'referent' in the same way that the law of contagion binds the Bible and God; the congregation's social order exists for sociological readers in the same way as God exists for the priest's audience. Both audiences are emotionally, physically and intellectually engaged in ritual performances of sacred cosmogony. My account ascribes the priest with magical capacities, but these are demonstrated through sociology's magical narrative and literary capacities. The Society created in this way necessarily carries the generally denied marks of textual forms, just as the

Sociologists and Anthropologists of these paragraphs carry the mark of my storytelling.

* * *

> if much of poetry, music and the arts aims to 'enchant' – and we must never strip that word of its aura of magical summons – much also, and of the most compelling, aims to make strangeness in certain respects stranger. It would instruct us of the inviolate enigma of the otherness in things and in animate presences. Serious painting, music, literature or sculpture make palpable to us, as do no other means of communication, the unassuaged, unhoused instability and estrangement of our condition. (Steiner 1989: 139)

Sociology, history and anthropology have all been traditionally motivated by a horror of disorder. Social analysis is often a story of the heroic quest into chaos from which the analyst emerges with order. To make their achievement seem the greater, all three disciplines emphasise the dangers they encounter and the strangeness they strive to tame. History deals with our murky past, when people believed the world was flat, when witches flew, when kings had power by divine right. Anthropology deals with foreign societies, often taken as markers of an evolutionary past, where ancestral spirits are worshipped and people believe in magic. Distanced from the exotic, sociologists anxiously compensate by showing the strangeness of everyday life in western societies. These forms of strangeness are the trouble that social analysis strives to resolve, through explanations that provide the emotional security of endings.

A major issue raised in this book is whether there might be sociological ways of knowing that forgo a masterful assimilation of the foreign. Although analyses promising a complete order are often prized, they are a megalomaniac's fantasy, less honest, rigorous and empirically accurate than analyses that offer more fragmentary, suggestive and overtly literary approaches. It is not that the former have *found* a complete or objective point of view, it is that they hide their ignorance and the specificity of their knowing. Narrativity is one such specificity, and I have suggested that narrative structures used in social analysis are far from neutral, far from natural. All narrative shares myth's powers of the divine, but despite being as awesomely creative as the verses of Genesis, sociology rarely acknowledges either its reliance on stories or the meanings generated through narrative form.

The reason for this silence may be sociology's institutional promise of an enlightened knowledge that explains (away) wonder, that demystifies the dark space of myth, that replaces emotion with intellect. Nevertheless, sociology could adopt a different relation to wonder, appreciating that even the most positivist sociological explanations are enchanted realignments of feelings and understandings. Scientific rigour cannot offer direct access to the real or eliminate the distance between self and other, but it can help us understand how we create what we feel we know. As Lévi-Strauss (1966: 225) put it, wisdom involves living myths seriously while remembering that they *are* myths. The strangeness that sociological explanation would eliminate is renewed at a different level in the very explanation.

Writing

How can one not dream while writing? It is the pen which dreams. The blank page gives the right to dream. (Bachelard 1971: 17)

to be able to dance with one's feet, with concepts, with words: need I still add that one must be able to do it with the pen too – that one must learn to write? (Nietzsche 1976: 513)

Dreaming and dancing with the pen; the pen dreaming. Such ideas would seem strange to a discipline that concerns itself with providing a clear account of social reality. Bachelard asks 'How can one not dream while writing?', and yet most forms of academic writing repress any notion of dreaming. I want to suggest that this repression of dreaming is effected through the repression of *writing* itself. It is not simply dancing and dreaming that are ignored in sociology lectures, it is pens too. The strangeness of these quotations comes not only from their metaphoric quality, but from their linking of the metaphoric and the imaginative with the practice of writing. In doing so they highlight this chapter's concern: how, indeed, to make the pen dance?

Writing and reading are seldom discussed by sociologists even though they are central to a sociological labour process. This is especially curious in the light of the prominence given to analyses of other labour processes. Sociologists might talk about the labour process at a Parker pen plant or an IBM plant; they might talk about the use of computers in the production of cars or even the implications of computers for the media industry. It would be most unusual, however, to find a sociological account of the use of pens or computers as tools in our own labour process. (Can computers dance? Is it the cursor that dances? Or is it our fingers on the keyboard that dance? What a different relation the hand, fingers, have to a pen and to a computer. I could never hold a pen lightly; my fingers, always messy with ink, squeezed it, my writing a sort of scratching of physical effort.) Yet writing *is* sociology's material labour process, involving furniture, rooms, rituals, equipment, paper, work relations and disciplines, the development of skills, negotiations of public and private life, rules of essay writing or article writing, publishing practices, and physical and psychic states of the writing subject or intellectual worker. Writing is a generally solitary activity, but it is still thoroughly material and social. Why, then, are the materiality and sociality of writing not talked about?

Sociological writing takes itself to be transparent: it provides a clear account. Writing must not get in the way of a representation of social reality. By drawing attention to the reality of the medium, the materiality of writing makes it difficult to avoid the productive or constitutive character of writing. As in other labour processes, transformations are effected; one does not end up with the same material – meaning – as one started with. But to acknowledge that writing is involved in the production or transformation of meaning is to acknowledge that sociological writing – and hence knowledge – is a cultural production. Here we touch upon a central concern of this book. If sociological writing denies itself, it does so because there are things at stake in terms of its status as knowledge: a pretension to Truth is retained by a fantasy of standing outside, of not partaking of the material world which one would know. The materiality of knowledge, a central aspect of which is writing, is denied in order to retain a privileged status of knowledge, which in the case of sociology is usually defined as science.

Now we can begin to glimpse (how easily we slip into metaphors of sight, the very metaphors that invite notions of the transparency of the world) something of the connections between the materiality and the creativity of writing. It is not too difficult to move from the constitutive character of writing to an understanding of writing as an imaginative, creative process. And this is what stands at odds with any understanding of knowledge as representation; as most sociologists see it, we are moving into the domain of fiction here, away from (social) science. It seems to me that it is not accidental that writers who speak about the materiality of writing – often the most profane and prosaic aspects of it – are those who value creativity. In the context of the opening quotation, Nietzsche is talking about the need to develop the skills to think–write–dance; Bachelard speaks of himself as an 'intellectual workman' (1971: 51), yet claims that a major part of this work consists of dreaming or 'reverie' (see also Barthes 1991: 177–82; Calvino 1993: 93–126). What, then, are the implications for sociological practice if we take dreaming and imagination seriously? What are the implications for the sociological work of writing?

* * *

> science will become literature insofar as literature . . . is already, has always been science; for what the human sciences are discovering today, in whatever realm . . . literature has always known; the only difference is that literature has not *said* what it knows, it has *written* it. (Barthes 1986: 10)

What is the import of 'has *written* it' in this quotation? Something is being said about different forms of writing – scientific and literary – and the connections between forms of writing and understandings of knowledge and truth. There is a suggestion that scientific writing is not 'writing'. What is at issue here is the connection between language and knowledge. Barthes claims that science is scandalised by language's integral role in knowledge (1986: 10).

'Writing' and the related ideas of 'reading' and 'text' have become almost everyday terms in some areas in the humanities, in literary theory, cultural theory and analysis, but not in sociology. The simple but important point made in contemporary theory is that these terms draw attention to the fact that we are in language. As metaphors for knowledge practices, they imply that language is not a transparent medium for conveying facts, concepts or indeed the self: these are not given, or prior to language, or expressed in language. Thus too it makes a difference if knowing subjects are thought of, and experience themselves, as writers or observers or scientists. Another way of putting this would be to say that facts, concepts and the self are culturally produced.

Writing unsettles the assumption that scientific language is a neutral instrument of thought, and hence normal, while other languages such as the poetic and the literary are ornamental, decorative deviation (Barthes 1986: 8; see also Calvino 1989: 28–34).

For literature, in contrast to science, thought is inseparable from language; 'writing' is aware of itself as language. Certainly what Barthes says about science rings true for much sociological writing which regards itself as a scientific representation of reality, and hence not writing (*that* is for fiction). Notions of truth in sociology are connected with the idea of a reality that is a presence, there to be represented: a sociological text is the transparent bearer of the truth of the world. Barthes refers to 'the fiction of a theological truth . . . disengaged from language' (1986: 10), claiming that only 'writing can break' with the 'paternal terror' of scientific truth (1986: 9). Writing disturbs 'reality', and any truth grounded in reality; it also disturbs the notion of an objective observer, outside social relations (Barthes 1986: 7–8). The only reality we can discuss is culturally produced. And the scholar – one who uses language – is *in* language, the sociality of language; the scholar is culturally produced.

It will have emerged by now that we are talking about two dimensions of writing, what might commonly be understood as the literal and the metaphoric: writing in the narrower sense of a specific form of signification or medium, and writing in the broader sense of cultural production (Clifford and Marcus 1986). Why is it that in contemporary theory writing has become the specific medium that is metaphoric of cultural mediations and productions more generally? This prompts the further question: what happens to common understandings of 'literal' writing in the course of this metaphoric transfer?

In contemporary work on writing, particularly that associated with Derrida and Barthes, there is constant movement between these dimensions of writing. This play with writing is central to Derrida's critique of notions of the presence of meaning to consciousness. He emphasises the written of language over the spoken, or 'the writing within speech', in order to reverse what he takes to be a privileging of speech associated with the desire for presence: I am speaking, speaking the concept, expressing myself, I am present unto myself, and present also to you, to whom I speak. In this understanding of language, speech is regarded as natural and authentic, and writing is a representation of speech; writing can be an accurate representation, but within it lie the possibilities of deviation and decoration – impurity. That writing is constituted in this way suggests that there is something potentially threatening about it: what is excluded as decoration – the metaphoric – unsettles notions of truth based on presence. In Derrida's view, writing is repressed because it threatens presence (1978: 197).

At one level this argument is based on the rather obvious observation that the substance of the medium of writing does not, so easily as speech, allow for notions of immediacy and transparency (Derrida 1987: 25). A crucial aspect of the repression is that writing comes to be defined as superfluous to the authentic of language. Thus the materiality of writing is repressed (which prompts one to think about what of speech must also be repressed to maintain a notion of *it* as a transparent medium – the materiality of the body speaking, the voice). To question the privileging of speech is, then, to demand 'a new concept of writing', an approach to writing based on different assumptions about meaning or signification than those which inform a 'metaphysics of presence' (Derrida 1987: 7–8, 26–7). (It must surely, then, produce a different concept of speech as well.) In this view, writing specifically and signification more generally are understood as processes of transformation rather than representation.

Derrida's point about transformation is an important one, but the case for writing over speech seems to be overstated: both writing and speech can invite fantasies of presence. A more interesting project would involve developing an appreciation of the ways in which speech and writing work differently as signification systems, and the various ways in which they relate to and affect each other. Consider, for example, forms of writing in which one can feel speech, can hear the voice, writing which provokes the desire to speak it, as so often happens with pleasurable texts. Do we not want to speak poems out loud, to hear our voice, feel our body speaking them? This is not about a desire for self-presence but a desire for performance, a bodily performance of language.

The critique of presence makes problematic the very distinction between the literal and the metaphoric. Is it possible, then, to retain the idea, basic to the social sciences, of a written language stripped of the embellishments of metaphor to produce a clear meaning, a clear account of social reality? If we accept this critique, writing in the narrower sense becomes inseparable from writing in the broader sense of cultural production: when we write with our pens, our computers, we are engaging in cultural production rather than merely representing a reality that is given, providing the literal meaning of that reality. Thus we return to the idea that there is no writing outside the metaphoric, that writing and writer are themselves metaphoric and are thought or experienced metaphorically. And if this is the case, the metaphoric is not 'merely' so – the metaphoric is literal.

It might seem somewhat paradoxical to be speaking about the denial of writing when in a rather obvious way writing is the privileged form in universities and western culture more generally. In the evaluation of both students and staff, writing is given precedence over oral, visual, performative media; it is principally essays and publications which count. Even in music and film departments, composition and performance do not, as a rule, have the same value as publications for purposes of promotion. It might also be objected that there is something Eurocentric in Derrida's emphasis on writing, and the predominance of the idea that the world is written, over, for example, ideas that it is sung, painted, danced (Lévi-Strauss 1976: 385–99). These are important critical questions, and there is obviously nothing necessary about the dominance of writing. But insofar as it is this way, the issue is what we make of this medium, how we might use its possibilities.

The central Derridean point remains: the repression of writing as transformation is the other side to the privileging of writing as representation. What is said on promotion committees is that performance and fictional texts are creative and thus more difficult to evaluate objectively than representational pieces; it's all just a matter of subjective likes and dislikes where creativity is concerned. Traditional academic criteria of evaluation are thus destabilised by understanding writing as creative rather than representational. Thinking of writing in these terms invites questions about the creative potentialities of different forms and the possible relations between these and writing. In short, once writing is understood as transformation, the way is open to put into question its dominant position.

* * *

If sociological writing is a form that denies itself, there are, nevertheless, rules for this writing, codes for clear scientific writing.

Students' hesitations in taking up invitations to *write* suggest that, at least intuitively, they know this. Bachelard speaks of the blank page giving the right to dream, but I suspect this is not a common experience for students. The clean sheet is so often faced with an anxiety invoked by a sense of the invisible authority of academic law. 'The paternal terror of Truth': will I speak the truth, in the name of the disciplinary Fathers? And what if I should stray? Have I got the correct thoughts together that will now be transcribed onto the page that awaits?

Even if not made explicit, the rules of sociological writing usually require a 'neutral', non-literary form that denies that form constitutes meaning. And yet this is itself an acknowledgement that form is implicated in meaning, for literary forms are rejected on the assumption that they will constitute non-sociological meanings. Here, for example, is an exchange between two examiners of an honours thesis. The first marker began her report by saying 'This is a lovely thesis'. The second marker agreed with this description but used it to contend that the thesis was non-sociological. If a piece of writing was 'lovely', it must be literature. Moreover, this marker went on, the first marker had confirmed the point by positively valuing the storytelling aspects of the thesis. Where were the facts? The argument? The general sociological conclusions?

The central point here is that science's genre of transparent writing constitutes social reality in a particular way, as, for example, consisting of facts. It also constitutes the relation between itself and that reality in a particular way – as a relation of separation, distance. One of the alleged problems with the 'lovely' honours thesis was that it was a (moving) story of the research relation between the 'researcher' and her 'informant'. It never left a position of 'being part of'. Scientific writing constitutes itself as not only outside, but also as non-constitutive; it desires to be invisible but must draw attention to itself to enforce the prohibitions that students know so well.

Calvino could be speaking of sociologists when he says:

The eyes of philosophers see through the opaqueness of the world, eliminate the flesh of it, reduce the variety of existing things to a spider's web of relationships between general ideas. (1989: 39)

For sociologists also value abstractions over lived experience and generalisations over particularity. And it comes across in the writing; a transparent writing, as Calvino so subtly implies, produces the world as transparent and as disembodied. All that's left is a world comprised of a few general patterns, or even a single dynamic, of, say, rationalisation. This reduction is the sociological achievement. There are no nuances, no complexities, no signs of confusion or unclear thought. The form of writing is, in turn, closely connected with rules about the structure of a piece of writing, the point of connection in sociological writing being 'an argument', a clear argument which produces the general patterns in all their transparency.

The traditional structure of a thesis – and an essay is a version of this structure – consists of the following elements, considered necessary to a sociological argument: introduction, methods chapter, theory chapter, presentation of data, development of argument, conclusion. Such a structure is based on representational assumptions about writing: there is method in the collection of the data, social facts; theory provides an interpretative model for ensuring an accurate representation of the facts. These two aspects are considered separately: the facts to be collected, on the one hand, and the representation of them, on the other. (During postgraduate reviews, students working in this genre will say: 'I have done the methods chapter and data collection, but haven't done the theory chapter yet; I haven't decided what theory to use.')

The inseparability of concepts and language ensures that research is writing right from the start. As Barthes says, it is fiction that 'research is reported but not written' (1986: 70). Engaging in a research practice, we are engaging in cultural production. This idea also has very important practical implications for the literal of writing. I will say more about this in the following section.

So what are the characteristics of *writing*? In a way this whole book is about the possibilities of alternatives to transparent social science writing. *Writing* is passionate. It is a form of writing that retains the quality of lived experience, carries with it something of that which is being written about. It is a form of writing that 'consents to remain metaphorical' (Barthes 1977: 156). And a writing that acknowledges the place of dreaming.

Most importantly, *writing* invites us to take pleasure in academic practices of reading and writing. Because of the demand
for representation, sociology students rarely associate writing
with pleasure, but once the connection between thought and
writing is recognised, pleasure is possible. For then we write not
to present a Truth but to discover how we think. And in this
process a pleasure in ideas and a pleasure in writing become
intimately connected.

In 'From Science to Literature', Barthes questions the basis of
Coleridge's differentiation of poetry from science in terms of pleasure and truth respectively (1986: 9). This, Barthes says, is to
trivialise pleasure and vacate the territory of truth. Thus, Barthes
unsettles a distinction between poetry and science and disturbs
the presumptions of science to truth. Implicit in this is a notion of
a poetic, metaphoric truth, and, I think, a truth in pleasure. For
sociological practice, it would be a matter not of choosing
between science and poetry, but rather being open to a play with
writing genres and the possibilities for knowledge that are
opened up by the poetic (see also Berger 1984: 22).

* * *

Students often seem peculiarly resistant to the suggestion that
writing is a skill that requires daily practice. I suspect many
believe writing is merely the form in which scholars report
research and express thoughts. But if research is writing, there are
serious practical implications to consider. If writing is a form of
creation, we need to write continually. And of course this is not
simply a practical question. It is through writing that ideas get
developed: thinking with the pen.

There is more to the mediations and materiality of writing than
language. A lot of what is involved in writing would commonly
be regarded as peripheral, and yet 'the peripheral' makes writing
possible. Take the most familiar example, the rituals in preparation for getting to the desk. Although often considered neurotic,
or avoidance mechanisms, these may be necessary preconditions
for the process of writing. Perhaps they would be better understood as part of the writing.

Preparation rituals are often rituals of separation and differentiation. I cannot write unless my bed is made and the dishes

washed. These separating activities are part of the process of getting to the desk; I would feel lost without them. They make
writing possible. In an essay on the purification ritual of putting
out the rubbish, Calvino says that 'through this daily gesture I
confirm the need to separate myself from a part of what was once
mine', a part of our being 'must daily sink away . . . so that
another part of our being may remain' (1993: 103–4).

> Writing, no less than throwing things away, involves dispossession,
> involves pushing away from myself a heap of crumpled-up paper
> and a pile of paper written all over. (Calvino 1993: 125)

Calvino is writing about rubbish and writing, the relation
between which is both metaphoric and metonymic – writing
scraps and food scraps must be removed in order that he might
go on writing (and, indeed, eating). While there might be an element of fantasy in the separation of which Calvino speaks, this
story of his experience tells us something about the everyday rituals of writing.

In saying a little here about my experience of writing I am not
suggesting that it is or should be the same for everyone, and I
would warn against attempts to apply anything like a formula.
But I do think that hearing about others' experiences can help the
writing and contribute to a demystification.

Writing allays panic for me, calms anxiety; it is a grounding
experience. This does not mean that it is easy, simply that if I am
not in a routine of writing I feel panic, something of me is miss-
ing. When I *am* in a writing routine, solitude can be intensely
pleasurable. The relation with oneself, one's writing, can also be
driven, frenzied (Bachelard 1971: 51; Nietzsche 1976: 518). Maybe
a sort of balancing goes on between obsession and 'being at ease'
with myself. Getting close to this is possible in moments when life
is devoted to writing in a rather singular way. I have in mind here
periods of leave from teaching and administration, when there is
no externally imposed time-discipline, and writing is the central
work activity. Part of the pleasure of this is control over one's
time, self-discipline and organisation of everyday life activities. In
turn, I think this self-discipline enables creativity.

Reading is a discipline that we use as a prelude to writing. As
a rule there is a clear point where I leave reading and begin to

write (see Bachelard 1971: 17), a point when reading has given me such energy that I can no longer not write, when further reading without writing would dissipate my energy. I choose carefully what I will read at this stage: writers who set me off, provoke the desire to write. (In the case of this chapter, Bachelard, Barthes and Calvino have clearly figured quite centrally.) So reading is about a relation with writers that makes another writing possible. (Just as writing is about a relation with readers – an issue addressed in *Managing*.)

Once 'writing' begins, I don't stop reading, but I am immersed in my writing. It has taken over. In these phases I live what I am writing all the time, feeling it as a 'jumping out of my skin'. I am, in a sense, writing all the time, whatever activities I might be engaged in. This is more than just thinking about what I am writing; it is a living of the materiality of that writing.

I have obviously differentiated activities within 'writing'. The moment referred to above is nowadays the moment of switching on the computer. Earlier I said that we write all the time, and the point is exemplified by the fact that I start every day (teaching and administration days, holiday days) with a reading–writing activity. Perhaps this is best described as a thinking activity that takes the form of reading–writing: a thinking, through a process of reading–writing. It seems necessary to me to go through this morning (prayer) ritual as a way of starting the day, getting the rest of the day right (Bachelard 1971: 26). But I don't experience this as duty; it is pleasure in an ascetic sort of way. Furthermore, this daily activity of thinking through writing, making scrappy notes that go in manila folders or notebooks, makes possible that moment when the 'writing' takes over. ('Takes over' is how it feels – I can't make it happen, it just comes.)

I want briefly to mention the other activities that I combine with writing during periods of concentrated writing. For example, in writing my last book, I spent the morning writing, the afternoon walking, riding or swimming, and the evening, when in an urban space, eating and drinking with friends. Walking, riding and swimming are not experienced as mere relaxation; they are forms of movement necessary to thinking, building up a rhythm for writing. But I would also say that I am writing while I am moving. When I get home, I will have already done some editing and written the next paragraph. The converse is true too:

writing is a movement, and when writing, I am walking, swimming or riding. Activities that are in a metonymic or contiguous
relation with each other become metaphoric.

* * *

> poets prefer to forget that while they write they are writing and not
> doing something else. Through more than three hundred sonnets,
> Petrarch pretends to believe he is walking in the open countryside,
> overwhelmed by suffering and anguish, whereas he is actually seated
> comfortably in his study, his cat on his lap. (Calvino 1989: 292)

Calvino is not advocating that writers stick to the literal of writing or think of writing in and of itself as writing. It would be fair
to say that for him there is no literal outside the metaphoric.
His interest is in a reflexive writing, a writing that is aware of
itself, and that acknowledges the figurative. In contrast to
Petrarch's country walks, Calvino cites Cavalcanti, who wrote a
sonnet in which the pens and other writing tools address the
reader. Are pens speaking any less metaphoric than writers
walking simply because we imagine the hand holding the pen?
No. And indeed Calvino positively values a writing which
includes 'the countless and multiform ways in which pens and
pencils and brushes can portray pens and pencils and brushes'
(1989: 291–9). These ways must be ways of contrast, difference or
divergence (1989: 294–5): pens and pencils are never just that.
And nor is writing.

   Like words, any activity only takes on meaning in relation to
another activity. We never just write or eat or walk or cook, but,
rather, we experience these activities through relations of difference and similarity with other activities. If no term or word
stands alone, this is true of writing. Metaphors or figures for the
writer and writing make writing possible: writing is actualised
through the living of these metaphors. Here we come back to
dreaming, the operations of the imagination: in dreaming of
walking while writing do we not enact it, make it alive, live the
image of walking? This points to how we might understand the
materiality of imagination: this dreaming will surely have an
effect on the quality of the writing, the form, rhythm, flow, the
feel (see Bachelard 1983: 1-18; see also Berger 1984: 22).

One has to get going. This is what writing is, starting off. It has to do with activity and passivity. This does not mean one will get there. Writing is not arriving; most of the time it's *not arriving*. One must go on foot, with the body. One has to go away, leave the self. How far must one not arrive in order to write, how far must one wander and wear out and have pleasure? (Cixous 1993: 65)

Writing is an apparently sedentary activity, but it also moves. It is a medium in which temporality has a rather obvious place. Writing, we move from word to word, sentence to sentence, setting forth without knowing where or how our writing–journey will end. Figures of the writer and writing are, most commonly, figures of movement. How they move matters. There are forms of movement in which everything stands still, nothing moves, so to speak; other forms are mobile, effect transformations. So, to bring this discussion back to a practical level, there is going to be a connection between the form of movement in the figures of our dreaming and the quality of the writing.

One of the most familiar metaphors for writing is walking. 'Only thoughts reached by walking have value' (Nietzsche 1976: 471). In contemporary theory a particular way of walking, the stroll, wandering, has come to figure prominently as metaphoric of *writing* and indeed 'writing the body' (Barthes 1977: 159; Cixous 1993: 64–5). The stroll is to be distinguished from the linear purposive walk of representational writing. Whereas the latter walk is concerned only with a goal, the stroll is a writing that is a 'not arriving'. Purposive walking denies the mediations of the walk itself, the differences, transformations, effected in the process of walking. An abstract walk, it could be any walk. On the other hand, particularity and qualitative difference are the essence of wandering. To put this another way, whereas the linear purposive walk is already mapped out, and then simply walked, represented, written up, the stroll is written in the process of walking.

Benjamin's account of Baudelaire's strolling *flâneur* has become popular in contemporary cultural theory. However, although the *flâneur* is the most familiar of Baudelaire's figures of modernity, Benjamin claims that the metaphor of the fencer is more apt as a self-portrait. He makes reference to Baudelaire's view that it takes a lot of will-power and hard work to be creative: for Baudelaire, 'poetic work resembled a physical effort' (Benjamin 1973: 67). The artist engaged in a duel '*stabs away* with his pencil, his pen, his brush' (1973: 68). Benjamin quotes Baudelaire: 'I go practising my fantastic fencing all alone, scenting a chance rhyme in every corner, stumbling against words as against cobblestones, sometimes striking on verses I had long dreamt of' (1973: 68). For Baudelaire, creative activity is a combination of dreaming, daydreaming and physical effort.

In Nietzsche too we find figures of struggle, physical effort in the will to power: Zarathustra walks, he walks in the winds, high in mountain winds. As Bachelard says, 'walking is his battle', and it is this that produces his 'rhythmic energy' (1983: 161–2). But Zarathustra doesn't just walk: 'Now I am light, now I fly, now I see myself beneath myself, now a god dances through me' (Nietzsche 1976: 153). And, to return to the passage from which I took my opening quotation: in *Twilight of the Idols* thinking–writing is referred to as 'like dancing, *as* a kind of dancing' (Nietzsche 1976: 512). This ever so slight change in formulation says an awful lot about how metaphors work: writing *is* a dancing. Metaphors want to be taken literally.

The walker, the fencer, the dancer; I could add the swimmer, in anticipation of issues that will be raised later in the book about fluidity (Bachelard 1983: 163–71), but instead I will say a little about another of my figures – the rider:

'O where are you going?' said reader to rider. (Auden 1976: 60)

I am interested in bringing together two of my passions (obsessions?), riding and writing. There are, of course, very different experiences of riding, and I want to make a distinction here between wild riding over moors and the disciplined riding of dressage. For some, writing is wild:

We must write at the dictation of our master the dream, a pencil in hand, straddling the mane at full gallop. (Cixous 1993: 107)

This sounds wonderful, but in fact it is dressage that I will talk about here. (Although I'm wondering as I write this if a bit more wildness in my writing might not be in order.)

Dressage, or classical riding, involves the combination of

discipline and freedom. Discipline makes a freedom of movement possible. Attaining perfection in movement takes hard
work and dedication. There is no doubt that this work is about
mastery, mastery of one's own body, the horse's body and, most
importantly, the relation between them – that is what *riding* is.
What makes the rider different from the walker or the swimmer
is the relation with another living being, for the well-known ideal
of riding is the unity of horse and rider (on the centaur, see
Bachelard 1971: 31). Whatever we might think of notions of unity,
this is a unity in which it would be difficult to erase difference,
and this is surely the pleasure of it. Sceptics will immediately
point to the human domination and mastery of difference
involved. Nevertheless, I think there is something in this being a
living relation. The relation between the rider and the horse in
movement is perhaps what I think of as metaphoric of the relation of the writer to the writing: and, thus, the writing might
come alive.

The aim of riding is to produce in the horse a freedom of movement, balance, rhythm, cadence, lightness. This is described as
feeling like flying (at its best the horse's feet barely touch the
ground), sometimes like dancing. The rider brings out the potential in the horse with neither force nor a simple operation of the
intellect. It works by living a movement in one's body (which
certainly has an intellectual component) and transmitting it to
the horse. But in order to live a movement, one has to understand how a horse moves, and this horse in particular. There is a
return, an exchange, a reverberation perhaps. The ideal of dressage is the realization of the potential in our body, in the horse's
body; it involves an energy in a relation between two bodies.

Dancing with the pen may make us think of the hand, and
hands are also a crucial link between rider–writer and the horse:
'your hands, that's how you talk to your horse'. One neither
blocks nor pulls with hands, but, rather, rides a horse into them
(impulsion is what matters, a going forward); so, she is in one's
hands, in giving, soft hands. Even restraining hands give. If we
block ourselves, we block the horse, we block our writing. And
the only way one can acquire this language of the hands is
through 'the feel'. It cannot be taught, or communicated, in any
abstract way, but must be lived in our bodies. And this is a skill:
it is precision with one's hands that makes all the difference.

Rhythm, cadence, a musicality to riding. We advise students to read drafts of essays and thesis chapters for the rhythm; passages that might be reworked can be identified by the loss of rhythm – just as, I might say, you can feel the loss of rhythm in a horse. Thinking about figures of the writer, then, has quite practical implications. By inviting critical reflection, figures can help us change our writing practice and develop our writing skills. Thinking about the figures that we write to encourages us to address our motivations in writing. It can also, quite simply, be inspiring. Our identifications with figures tells us something about the nature of our relation to our writing, or, to put this another way, the constitution of the writing self.

* * *

Where is the self in the writing? This is a controversial and complex question which will be addressed in *Reading* in terms of how 'the author' figures in readings of texts. We can begin here by considering the differences in assumptions about the self in representational writing and *writing*. In 'From Science to Literature', Barthes suggests that scholars who constitute themselves as 'writers' unsettle the subjective–objective distinction that is so basic to our common understandings of knowledge (1986: 7–8). The self is absent from representational notions of writing; the subject of scientific transparent writing is a disembodied, external objective consciousness. If the materiality of the writing is not acknowledged, nor is that of the writing self. A representing objective consciousness is in a sense outside culture, unlike the material subject of transformative writing, who is in the writing, and in culture.

The formulation 'we are written' has become a commonplace way of saying that we are culturally produced. It stands in contrast to an expressive model of writing or language: the notion that, say, in writing we are expressing a pregiven self, an identity, or representing a self-presence. But this should not be read in an idealist sense to suggest that since the self is produced in language, 'the self' somehow disappears; it is the self of self-presence that disappears with *writing*. Nor should it be taken to mean that the self is simply written in a passive manner, that the self is a blank sheet to be written on. In answer to such a conception of

pure perception Derrida has said 'we are written only as we write' (1978: 226). The 'only as we write' is absolutely crucial to an understanding of the relation between the self and writing. We would not be written, culturally produced, unless we wrote, were actively engaged in the process of cultural production, of ourselves.

And thus the idea of 'writing the self', an idea that has become familiar in cultural theory through the writings of people such as Barthes and Cixous. While representing the self implies a pre-given self that is expressed in the writing, *writing* involves a becoming of the self, a making of a self that is not already all of a piece, but, rather, is in process. In writing and other practices, then, there is the potential for self-transformation; the self is a wandering self, in a state of permanent becoming. Foucault speaks of the ideal of creating ourselves, our lives, as works of art: a 'practice of creativity – and not of authenticity' (1984: 351), and Nietzsche insists on the passion in this process of becoming (1976: 560–3; see also Barthes 1975: 62).

The moving, writing self is a material self rather than a disembodied consciousness, and, thus, writing the self is connected with the idea of writing the body. Barthes speaks of 'the materiality of the body speaking' (1977: 182), and significance as meaning *'insofar as it is sensually produced'* (1975: 61). And once we think of the self in bodily terms, it is difficult to avoid our lived experience as sexed and sexual beings. If in writing we are writing the body, our sexual body must be there in the writing. Again, the very idea of writing undoes any fixity or pregivenness in sexuality, a sexual or sexed identity, presence. Barthes, Irigaray and Cixous have linked writing with a multiplicity in sexes and sexualities. Cixous, for example, associates writing with the feminine, with bisexuality, with ambiguous sexuality; she does so because these positions are other, but, more importantly, because they are open to otherness:

> Writing is the passageway, the entrance, the exit, the dwelling place of the other in me – the other that I am and am not, that I don't know how to be, but that I feel passing, that makes me live – that tears me apart, disturbs me, changes me, who? – a feminine one, a masculine one, some? – several, some unknown, which is indeed what gives me the desire to know and from which all life soars. (Cixous 1986: 85–6)

Creativity and imagination, in her view, require an abundance of the other in the writing self: a movement towards an other rather than an unveiling of an identity that's just there. How could this inspire dreaming, imagining? When we imagine, is it not something other? (Think of the way in which figures of the writer work through a process of identification involving both sameness *and* difference.) And is not imaginative writing the living of this otherness?

The difference between writing the self and representing the self can be understood perhaps in terms of the nature of the relation to the other. Representation assumes identity, a self-sameness; writing assumes a self never complete, but always in movement towards an other.

* * *

Cixous writes passionately. In the above quotation it is not simply that she is speaking about a writing motivated by a passionate relation to the other; she is *writing* that relation. We can feel the quality of the relation in the way she writes, in the rhythm and movement. Passionate writing is sensual, emotional; it retains 'the feel' and sense of life.

To give students a taste of writing the body, the pleasure in this, and the potential pleasure in the discipline of writing all the time, in short to inspire them to write, I often suggest they read Cixous or Barthes (particularly *The Pleasure of the Text*). My assumption is that an embodied form of writing is more likely to inspire students than an abstracted disembodied form. (This is not to suggest that Barthes and Cixous will work for everyone in the same way.) Scientific, representational writing would erase the affective and the sensual in knowledge and writing. It aims for a writing free of metaphor. It denies writing. Science calls upon scholars–students to forget their bodies, their emotions, and to aim for the heights of abstracted truth. This separation of intellectual life from practical life is likely to provoke terror (or possibly some feeling of power for being above life) rather than pleasure or a desire to get into writing. Non-emotional writing produces an affect, despite itself. There is something deadening, life-denying about this sort of writing. *Writing*, on the other hand, is conscious of itself as writing – as a creative material activity that enlivens, that is life-enhancing. Embodied writing allows us to experience language's potential for transmitting the quality of lived experience. Most importantly, passionate writing moves us, through its images, metaphors, rhythms. It moves us to dream, dream–read and write.

Ink

My 18-month-old child and I love poring over the pictures in his books to find where the mouse is, or the moose, or the moon. Recently I realised I had never asked him about one of the most conspicuous parts of the picture – the straight lines of black squiggles on almost every page. My eyes saw the printed text as words and sentences, not as black shapes on white paper, not as part of the picture, and I imagined my son could not see the text because he could not read the words. The word 'print' could not be more explicit – impress, stamp, mark, leave an impression – but still we treat print as a transitory medium that leaves no permanent mark on meaning. Writing and printing are invisible because we imagine they are a clear window onto our ideas rather than smudgy black ink on an opaque page. We fantasise that we communicate *through* writing instead of producing ideas *in* writing, as an artist may work *in* paint. Sociology pretends it is written in invisible ink.

As long as writing and print are invisible, academic writers can present themselves as 'mental' rather than 'manual' workers. Within existing caste discourses, this is a claim to labour market status, workplace autonomy and a spiritualised condition, placing professors at the very top of occupational status hierarchies, just below judges, alongside archbishops and above astronauts (Daniel 1983). Despite these privileges, many intellectual workers express regret for their alienation from the body. Sociologists often bemoan their estrangement from 'real work', where dirty hands get a true grip on the world. Many also regret their impracticality and then thank 'my secretary, Mrs X, for her invaluable help and patience', thereby both acknowledging and disowning the physicality of their work. These conspicuous regrets only draw attention to the purity of the writers' intellectuality, and we may assume that people who pen academic papers on this alienation don't really want to lose it. The same applies to those who won't receive the good news that their work *is* fully corporeal. Were sociological writing not physical, I wouldn't be worried about the writer's cramp in my left forearm; my publishers, though, might be worried that I had just produced and distributed these ideas telepathically.

Had we world enough and time, we might consider a range of sociology's media – the writing space of the computer screen, the difference between pen and keyboard, the voice of the lecture and the voices of the tutorial. Instead we'll take one example and consider some consequences of the fact that sociology is largely, but not entirely, an inky way of knowing.

* * *

In some ways the title of this chapter is a misnomer, for sociologists produce their works in white and black, page and ink. Although the unwritten page is conventionally seen as blank, it is not intrinsically so. It might be described as white paper, and white is full, the simultaneous presence of all colours, all possibilities. Paper usually seems this way before I mark it, when I'm abuzz with ideas that I could potentially get down. It is only as I steel myself to start, somewhere, somehow, now, it is only in the face of my desire for the white paper, that it becomes a barren and blank page. The same logic of desire led European settlers to say that the land that became Australia was empty – *terra nullius*. Before settlement, it had been white space on European maps – full of possibilities, a utopian space for dreams without limit. It only became empty in relation to colonial desires.

Far from erasing whiteness, writing is as bound to it as ink to paper. Consider the margin of a text, which is still white paper, but not normally thought of as empty page. It is not blank because it is full of meaning, signifying the end of the line of text, the frame separating the text from the profane world. As Butor notes, wide margins and thick leading in a book are a luxury, allowing readers more chance to dive into a text and their imaginations, secure from the profane world beyond the margins.

It is not happenstance that the paper in our books is white, always as white as possible, or that one of the most disturbing innovations of the Surrealists was their experimentation with printing on coloured paper. . . . The 'elsewhere' the book gives us appears, as we cross the page, to be penetrated with whiteness, baptised. Sometimes the refusal of the world as it is . . . become[s] so powerful that the reader prefers to remain suspended in the whiteness, calm at last. The 'elsewhere' that appears thanks to textual signs may now be considered only as an inundation of white light (1992: 55)

One of the reasons poetry is better equipped than prose for creating the specificity of a moment is that it uses typographical conventions and white paper to break up the written line, to bathe in cloistered stillness, to hold fragments in the magical space of the page. Lists also rely on typographical conventions, where white paper at once separates and connects items in a column.

When the white fullness of the margins and spacings is turned blank by the reader's desire to occupy and fix it, it can, however, become a space for readerly subversion of the 'black letter law'. Reading 'between the lines', people can claim to find what the ink doesn't say. Readers also challenge the writer's authority from the margins, like guerrillas fighting anti-colonial wars. In the margins of books they write their readings, showing a deeply scandalous disregard for the *cordon sanitaire* that protects authority. An inversion occurs when lecturers insist that the lack of wide margins on student essays is an impertinent refusal to cede teachers the space for their last word. The battle for scholarly authority wages in the margins of essays.

* * *

Writing is a form of travel across the space of the page. A key feature of conventional writing is its linearity. One word comes after another, just as one step comes after another. Readers following the inkily authorised route through this book progress from left to right, from top to bottom, and ideally from the first numbered page to the last. The significance of this obvious fact begins to emerge if you consider that a straightened text would be a long line of almost no width. Reading would be the one-way journey along this line. A sociology book might have 200 pages of text, 100,000 words, 500,000 letters, and extend for over a kilometre.

The reader's journey through writing is nicely expressed in the story that Jack Kerouac wrote *On The Road* on one continuous roll of paper, like toilet paper. Kerouac's story is about a journey from the east to the west of the United States: in theory at least, readers could traverse this path by unrolling his writing.

The linearity of text is also highlighted by reading's measurable speed. A quick reader with an easy novel may move at the considerable speed of 300 metres per hour. Moreover, when printers and publishers choose type sizes, typefaces, line widths and the amount of leading in the page, they are technologically regulating the reader's mood and speed. There are typefaces, type sizes and line widths that speed or slow the journey, that soothe the reader's eyes or keep them tense, that make readers feel relaxed or intimidated. Printers may build freeways or install visual speed humps.

This linearity is of profound significance, because neither experience nor contemplative thought comes naturally in linear form. Contemplation and experience may have no beginning point and no orderly sequence; they can involve simultaneities unavailable on the written line and much more complex patterns of interconnection than the line provides. Writing, then, is not the report of thought but the production of a specific type of thought and a specific account of life, distinct from the possibilities offered by painting, or dance, or speech. If writing weren't so dominant, we might not imagine thought coming naturally in lines of argument, with steps, signposts and backtracking. But *because* writing has become second nature to us, we often take its linearity as a reflection, rather than a likely source, of the alleged linearity of experience or thought. When I'm at my desk, pen in hand, trying to construct *lines* of argument, I often feel the frustration and failure of childhood art classes, when I couldn't make my drawings look perspectival, the way the world 'really was'. It helps to remember that my writing task is not to untangle what I'm thinking and feeling, it is to produce from it a particular – linear – form of thought. It is important not to lose sight of linearity's artifice and cultural specificity.

* * *

When writing is seen as linear movement across space, it becomes clear that people are moved both in and by writing and reading. There is a famous remark about Dante by the poet Osip Mandelstam:

> The question occurs to me – and quite seriously – how many shoe soles, how many ox-hide soles, how many sandals [Dante] wore out in the course of his poetic work, wandering about on the goat paths of Italy.
>   The *Inferno* and especially the *Purgatorio* glorify the human gait, the measure and rhythm of walking, the foot and its shape. The step, linked to the breathing and saturated with thought: this Dante understands as the beginning of prosody. (quoted in Chatwin 1988: 256)

Nadezhda Mandelstam develops this idea; although talking of long poems in particular, her point relates to prosody in general:

> [The works] we are speaking about always have a special momentum of their own which carries the reader along – as it has previously carried along the author – in an irresistible poetic surge, snatching him up like a wave, and setting him down again only at the very end, at the final pause. . . . [T]his 'momentum' constitutes the basic structural feature of a long work, giving it the quality of an uninterrupted river of verse with whirlpools, rapids, and crosscurrents, like any swift-flowing and not unduly shallow mountain stream. (1974: 424)

Movement within a text must therefore be analysed *as* movement, and not as a sequence of frozen positions. Like talking, bike-riding and other activities, writing and reading create poise by letting rhythm mobilise inherently unstable positions. They are deeply musical. Walking is a major source of human rhythm, providing an order so deep in our bodies and beings that even the smallest baby recognises its familiar caress. Rhythm organises writing and reading by walking us on, telling us when to breathe, telling us when moods intensify and slacken, telling us how to group words into phrases and clauses, involving our body in the movement of the text as if we were dancers moving in/to music. These movements *in* writing and reading are associated with the (e)motions produced *by* them.

Punctuation and parsing are the guardians of writing's music. The inky technology of the comma, the colon, the dash, the semicolon, the full stop, the new paragraph, the phrase, the subordinate clause: these are the bar lines and tempo markings of writing and reading, organising the movement of writers and readers through texts. Bad writing plods, drags, lurches, crawls, limps. Good writing sings and dances, or it races or marches or holds its breath. Good writers read well, listening to the melody of the words and the rhythms of the punctuation. Good writers also use these rhythms in the act of writing. The pen dances, the fingers on the keyboard fly. To feel the demands of rhythm, I often write to the accompaniment of some well-loved and deeply embodied music. When the writing flows it moves to the music.

The rhythms of walking/writing create spaces for different sorts of consciousness, including the un-self-conscious states prized by the many philosophers and poets who walk to work, by the Buddhists who follow their Master's injunction to 'walk on!', and by the Sufi dervishes who try to use the rhythm of end-less walking to become the Way itself (Chatwin 1988: 200). This un-self-conscious condition is what I most love about writing, reading and thinking, and often it relies on the micro-codes of punctuation. A full stop can be as emotionally satisfying as an ending is in narrative.

* * *

The print conventions in sociological writing are not limited to the line, margin and comma; conventions of chapter, section and part give structure to sociological writing and shape its meaning. Psychology and many natural sciences are explicit about the dis-ciplinary character of their formats, drilling first year students with the order in which 'reports' must be written. When these students later dismiss the relevance of the subject of writing, they show how habitual these codes have become. Although writing formats are rarely prescribed to sociology students, they never-theless worry that rules exist, albeit rules without codification or universal respect. Perhaps sociology lecturers don't broach the subject directly because they too are unsure of the rules or their rationale. Perhaps they think sociological writing too trivial to discuss. Or perhaps they sense that recognition of sociology's social conventions ultimately requires a reconstitution of the dis-cipline's modern image.

Because sociology should understand the meanings embedded

in (its) writing and publishing formats, we offer brief notes on some of the conventions that open most sociology books, including this one.

Title

Whether invented early or late in the writing, book titles strain to encompass the contents of developing texts. Nevertheless, because a title appears on the cover, it generates the impression that a book has a single point. It allegedly names the point and sets up an authorised basis for ranking themes and sub-themes and sub-sub-themes.

Many academic books use both a title and sub-title, separating the two with a colon. Thus G. Douglas Atkins' *Estranging the Familiar: Toward a Revitalized Critical Writing* (1992). There is an uneasiness about the way such titles combine an explicitly poetic phrase, usually coming first, with a more specific and 'literal' formulation. While these titles acknowledge the necessarily poetic operations of academic texts, the colon protects the literal from poetic contamination, allowing the subtitle to promise that the book's point could be identified literally if need be. Because it is a guarantee never tested, it is a guarantee easily made. The title and sub-title also establish the rhythm and melody of a question and answer. Atkins' title ascends to *Familiar*, where the colon cues a descension, culminating in *Writing*. This format is a movement from open to closed, the literal answering the problem of the poetic. A poetic sub-title, on the other hand, opens up an adventure.

Author

Authors are named on the cover and title page of books, and in the assertions of copyright and moral ownership often found on the imprint page. This claim rarely stands alone, however, calling for necessary supplementation and qualification in the imprint page, the dedication and the acknowledgements (see below).

Authorship is usually taken to imply the presence of a single viewpoint and voice whose coherence binds the disparate parts of the text with *a* meaning which the reader must locate. The Ern Malley literary hoax in Australia relied on the 'gullibility' of readers who dutifully found a coherence in the poems of the fictitious Mr Malley, writings that the hoaxers later claimed were scraps randomly compiled.

As pseudonyms indicate, authorship is far more problematic than the conventional wisdom allows. Readers of novels are often warned against mistaking narrators for authors, but in sociology a different problem prevails, for the narrator's voice is normally heard distinctly only in the 'prelim pages' that precede the proper text. In the rest of the text, no one in particular speaks. This impersonal writing style is so precious to academic knowledge that most students are strictly prohibited from using the term 'I' in their essays. Rhetorically this taboo implies that the essay or book deals in thought abstracted from all particularities, allowing the tacit implication that Knowledge or Reason or Modernity is speaking through the spirit-medium of the writer.

Because this implication is a bullying fantasy, I often use 'I' in this book. This 'I' establishes a narrator, but does not make 'me', the writer, who may or not have a painful forearm, any closer to immediate presence. Nor is 'I' used in the hope that I can cut through rhetoric with direct speaking. For one thing, am I the I or the 'I' of the previous sentence? Moreover, as reader, you will participate in the meaning of my 'I'. My 'I' is beyond my control, just as the author-function 'Borges' was beyond the control of the author Borges:

> The other one, the one called Borges, is the one things happen to. . . . I know of Borges from the mail and see his name on a list of professors or in a biographical dictionary. . . . Years ago I tried to free myself from him and went from the mythologies of the suburbs to the games with time and infinity, but those games belong to Borges now and I shall have to imagine other things. Thus my life is a flight and I lose everything and everything belongs to oblivion, or to him. I do not know which of us has written this page. (1970: 282–3)

In this book, 'I' isn't a promise of presence but a rhetorical reminder of the particular positions from which I (we?) work.

Collective authorship highlights many issues that, in principle, apply to cases of single authorship. Some collective authors efface their difference and claim singularity by ascribing authorship to, for example, the Boston Women's Health Book Collective. Some famous text and reference books virtually efface authorship altogether by turning the author's name into part of the title. Anthony Giddens' *Sociology* may outlive him, becoming *Giddens' Sociology*, revised by someone else for a new generation of students. The immortality of the author here is a claim to an immortality of the book's authority; it has unleashed itself from the corruption of corporeal form. In the present book, we have neither effaced our individual names on the title page nor consistently replaced 'I' with 'we': readers are welcome to work with any differences between us.

As in all joint-authorships, our names on the cover give clues to our relationship. Had our names defied the alphabet, readers would probably assume that Metcalfe was the senior author, either doing most of the work or being the more institutionally powerful. In the event, readers must guess whether Game is senior or the issue of seniority is effaced through the arbitrariness of the alphabet. Far from causing annoyance, this margin of doubt is crucial to the operation of the authors' names, allowing academia to pretend to disdain the dynamics of power, prestige and career advancement, while still providing the information on which academic reputations are founded. Academic selection committees read authors' names as subtly as theologians read the Bible.

Prelim Pages

Publishers refer to a book's first pages as the 'prelim' pages. These are the pages not considered proper text – the title page, publishing details, dedication, contents page, acknowledgements, preface – and their ambiguity is branded on them in roman page numbers. The term 'prelim', short for 'preliminary', clearly indicates that these pages are a border crossing, a theatre foyer, a car idling before it moves, the liminary stage preparing readers for the journey that is itself liminal. They prepare readers to operate according to the laws and conventions that apply in the world they're entering.

Prelim sections often occupy dozens of pages. The 'proper' text takes so long to enter because writing requires ritual preparation to create the right reading environment, even if it subsequently disowns this supplementation. Academics refer to their elaborate footnotes, references and bibliographies as 'scholarly apparatus', and this term nicely recalls the theatrical hoists and pulleys needed if ideas are to appear to fly across the pages of books.

Publisher's Imprint Page

The cover, title page and imprint page identify the book's publisher, the latter also giving information about editions, ISBN numbers, legal rights and so on. A 'good' imprint is an invaluable imprimatur, impressing potential readers and academic selection committees and encouraging them to notice and appreciate the book and its author. Because the 'same' text issued by different publishers is not the same book, authors court the best publishers they dare approach.

Yet if people rarely overlook the imprint on the book's spine, they rarely look at the imprint page. This is the most embarrassed and discreet of all the prelim pages, appearing without title, in a small typeface and an uninviting layout. Do not notice me, it says, like a wallflower at a dance. But precisely because it calls out to be unnoticed, this page calls attention to the invisible visibility required of publishers.

Myths of authorial creativity and autonomy underestimate the publisher's role in book production. Publishers don't just await book proposals sent in the mail, they suggest marketable books to authors and specifically commission writers for books they've designed; they stipulate a book's length, target audience and so on; they negotiate rewriting in response to readers' reports and market considerations; they insist on certain titles and covers; they make a host of design and editorial decisions that may change the whole style of the writing; they have the book printed, promoted, marketed and distributed; and those few university presses that don't do all these things for profit must still consider cost recovery. The publisher's role highlights the commercial and inky character of sociology books, but publishers hide their role for fear of diminishing the sacred aura of authors and books. Authors and publishers tacitly conspire to persuade audiences that books are only written because authors have something important to say, that books are only published because knowledge or culture demands it, that publishers and publishing are transparent conduits between authors and readers. As a necessary prelim supplement to fantasies of 'the author', the imprint page is designed to be the page that isn't there.

Dedication

Dedications are a supplement to the singularity of authorship, either adding subject positions outside that of 'writer' (e.g. spouse, parent, child) or acknowledging those whose influence marks the present text.

Because dedications encourage readers to equate author and narrator, they enhance the narrator's plausibility as a character. Although I enjoy reading them for clues to my imaginary 'real' author, their placement and tone ensure it is a strangely voyeuristic experience, even though this private message has been published. Dedications often become coy when authors start to perform their private lives for imagined readers.

Epigraph

Like imprint pages, epigraphs are outside the proper text and written by someone who isn't the author. They operate as a motto, another attempt to fix the book's point. This repetition betrays the author's anxiety that unaided readers may not find 'the' point of the thousands of words stretched across space (an anxiety most conspicuous in the book's running heads).

While acknowledging the influence of the epigraph and epigrapher, narrators often imply the benediction and some of the authority of the epigrapher. Curiously, sociologists often seem to take their epigraphs from poets, novelists and philosophers rather than other sociologists. This could be a synecdochic display to impress readers of the cultural sophistication of the narrator/author and the book: the narrator/author knows more than she or he can say in this book alone. Alternatively it could remind us that much sociology has lost its capacity to inspire because it has choked the play of language.

Pithy and poetic, epigraphs are offered as a treat to tantalise the reader's palate. But as many diners know, these appetisers are often the most striking part of a meal. The sociological author's own voice often resonates most strongly in the epigraph, when using someone else's words.

Contents Page

The contents page sets out an itinerary for readers, to guide their readings by guiding the expectations through which they read. Novels typically lack contents pages, insisting that readers leave themselves entirely in the author's hands, but the contents pages and indexes in sociology books allow readers to make their own way through the book, to reorder or even skip chapters.

The itinerary of a contents page gives a feeling of authorial purpose and inevitable order, but writing itself is more often an exploration than a journey with itinerary, and order and clear purpose may have been distant until the moment the contents page was finalised. A writer may spend years on a text, but it is completed as a whole, simultaneously. When the last word is finalised, all words are; until then, none are. All the false steps of earlier drafts are erased with the last word. These, for example, are not the words I first used in this sentence; the writing of this chapter did not commence on what is its first page; I originally intended this paragraph for the second chapter (which has subsequently become the fifth chapter); you cannot tell if I am lying. Books make the work of writing disappear, they make order seem inevitable and predestined, and as a special effect, they create a sense of unfolding time. Contents pages make these hard-won qualities seem natural.

Preface and Acknowledgements

Prefaces and acknowledgements usually insist that author and narrator are one, identified through a description of his or her specific friendships, domestic arrangements, intellectual debts and allegiances, and so on. The prefatorial voice encourages the reader to like the imagined narrator/author, to establish a bond that lingers when the voice changes in the main text. Acknowledgements often admit what the title page denies, that no one can write a book alone, yet they are where 'I' proliferates, where the stories behind the story are told. The narratorial voice here is relaxed, homely, warm, distinct from the more abstract, disembodied 'I-less' voice of the title page and proper text.

Although appearing very early in the book, the use of past tense shows that acknowledgements are written very late, as a reward for the completion of the authorial journey. Accordingly they lack the danger and unresolved tension driving the body of the text. They're a celebratory feast, gratitude and communion flowing like wine. At the same time, however, authors may need acknowledgements sections to establish their credentials, to create a mood, to honour their patrons and tacitly claim their blessing, to sustain the networks they need to produce their books. Academics may enjoy reading acknowledgements for the pleasure of the company, but they also read them for clues to the book's disciplinary positioning. These clues allow authors to be swiftly located and assimilated.

Although ubiquitous, acknowledgements sections remain awkward. They are a reminder that the author is a particular person from a particular society, with the same specific hassles and foibles as everyone else. This reminder contaminates the claim in the proper text to a more abstract and possibly objective knowledge. The use of roman numerals indicates embarrassment as clearly as the colon in a double title. By keeping the prelims separate, roman numerals falsely imply that the inky apparatus of a book could in principle be eliminated.

* * *

Because qualities only emerge through comparisons, I will use a comparison of speech and writing to develop this chapter's

discussion of writing. Voice and hearing were once privileged in western knowledge practices, and speech remains a significant medium of sociological knowledge. Nevertheless, speech is increasingly treated as an adjunct of literacy, which is adopted as the measure of all knowledges. After spending lectures writing down the notes that academics read to them, many students spend tutorials reading papers to each other, in preparation for the written work that will assess their learning. Such lectures and tutorials may as well be replaced by written handouts and interactive computer programs. In the formal proceedings of sociological conferences, 'speakers' often read papers before distributing copies. Informally speech retains a major role in conferences, and university corridors, as the medium for the gossip by which the discipline imagines and disciplines itself, but the gossipy basis of academia is only acknowledged in gossip and illicit university novels.

There is a large literature(!) presenting the rise of literacy as the loss of speech's immediacy, but the differences between speech and writing need not be understood through Edenic fantasies. This book isn't embarrassed by its literacy, because writing suits our purposes and the alternatives are no more authentic. The point, rather, is to understand the choices made when the pen is taken up, to know the specific qualities of the knowledges that sociology creates. A brief comparison of speech and writing will highlight the latter's qualities.

Unlike writing, speech isn't normally organised around sentences or paragraphs. Consider this example of 'speech', taken from a research interview with an Australian politician. My transcription system inserts new lines for pauses, capital letters for proper names, and underlining for words spoken with special emphasis:

> but I think we've had a
> if you look at it in historic terms
> and ah one of the things that has happened here and it's very
>   valuable I think has been that tripartite <u>working</u> that's
>   gone on
> particularly in terms of restructuring
> um the Workplace Resources Centre the fact that uh there's
>   been
> really an ability for the Trades Hall Council

and Local Government and State Government to
work with the large employers
and while it's a not a rapid process it's certainly probably
　　　well in advance of a lot of other centres
and obviously we've had the crisis points that have
ah forced that process along
I mean the run down in numbers at the BHP over the last
　　　decade
the problems of the Dockyard closing down
the fact that ah the submarine contract didn't come here the
　　　fact that the process of the frigates
um has really forced us to
while there was an enormous amount ah of local
angst
and also enormous parochialism
I think it also is part of the process of reassessment of what
　　　was happening here

Transcribed, this 'speech' seems awkward and obscure, yet it is
quite effective on the tape-recording of the interview, where it is
structured and coloured by vocal tones, pauses, inflections and
accents. In the interview itself the speaker's voice was supple-
mented by gesture, eye-contact and body language, by the
contemporary context of the interview and by the dialogic relationship within it.

Sociological analyses of interviews usually hide the awkward-
ness of written speech by extensively modifying their
transcriptions to remove hesitations, repetitions, diversions and
false starts, to add punctuation, to impose a line of argument, to
standardise grammar, to choose spellings, to decide on the position of capital letters and emphases, to make guesses about the
meaning of mumbled words, to delete 'extraneous' comments
about coffee or the weather. Thoughtlessly patronising, these
amendments presume to 'clarify' the line of thought, 'fix' the
spelling, 'improve' the grammar, as if speech were second-rate
first-draft writing. The text is then presented without acknowledgement of its alterations or of the interpretation they involved.

Barthes refers to these substitutions as the embalming of
speech (1991: 3), for such transcriptions severely reduce speech's
vocal, gestural and contextual qualities. One could as well suggest that all the actors who've played Hamlet have produced the

same meaning because they've used the same script. My transcription method is unusual because it preserves some of speech's rhythms, but it still loses most qualities of speech and imposes many qualities of writing. A better alternative might be to license more artistic simulations of the speech's qualities in the foreign language of writing, but this course would require great writerly skills and most sociologists would in any case reject its overt artistry.

If interview transcription is so problematic, why do most sociologists do it so thoughtlessly? One reason relates to the technologies of mechanical reproduction. It is not conventional or profitable to publish sociological studies in the multi-media formats that would allow informants to speak for themselves, at least in edited videotape form. CD-ROM technology may change this, but many sociologists will resist this medium if its enhancement of the reader's creativity threatens their own authority.

Another reason for voice's neglect may be its reminder of sociology's sociality, of the personal networks, the gossip and the particular accents that constitute the discipline. Sociologists prefer to see their discipline in terms of Knowledge and its development in terms of historical destiny and intellectual progress.

Perhaps the main reason for the careless imposition of writing is that appreciation of spoken and gestural knowledges undermines the universal pretensions of written sociology. At the time of their delivery, for example, speech and gesture are local knowledges with particular accents, embedded in specific contexts and dialogic relations, given their inflections by specific bodies, having little chance of reproduction or circulation beyond the immediate community. It is a dangerous medium because it operates in the heat of particular moments but refuses to allow the said to be un-said.

While speech cannot be undone, and while it can be entirely convincing, leaving space for doubt in neither speaker nor listener, it remains an evanescent knowledge. Because of its occasional quality, speech is less binding than writing, and because it isn't permanently set down in letters and words, it cannot be tied to a literal meaning. Because the performance and reception of speech and gesture involve forgetting and not-noticing, speakers and listeners can neither preserve the performance for detailed scrutiny nor have second thoughts about elements of the performance unheeded at the time. Statements that glare with contradiction during analysis of a transcript may have seemed compatible during the original encounter because they were separated in time. Because of its remorseless flow, speech prohibits the backward reference needed to identify the precise relation between the incremental points through which it expands. These increments follow in time without necessarily following in abstract logic or leading to a conclusion. Finally, because speech and gesture are always overfull of meaning, two accurate witnesses could never offer identical reports, even with access to a record of the occasion. Some theorists argue that hearing is a warmer and less objective sense than the sight used in reading; whether or not it is, encounters between speaking and listening bodies involve a *range* of senses (sight and perhaps touch with gesture, sound with voice, perhaps smell with proximity) and the complex interactions between perceptions make it difficult to fix and singularise the experience or its meaning. Accordingly hearsay reports of someone's speech are given discounted credibility.

Sociological writing encourages abstraction with timeless and disembodied concepts and with the conventions of a dispassionate and impersonal narrator. But writing itself involves abstraction, written knowledge being neither as local nor as specific as spoken knowledge. Words written by a particular writer to a particular imagined readership will probably be read by other readers in different contexts, in terms of an imagined author. Writing 'speaks' to no-one and everyone, to now and the indefinite future. Printing presses may be reproducing the book in countries and centuries unknown to the author. Whereas speakers negotiate their interactions with audiences through body language and ritualised interpellations ('you know?', 'yes?', 'do you see what I mean?'), writers are only spectators by the time readers are appropriating the words once theirs:

> And then [the writing is] finished, and the great shock comes when it's printed! . . . What was once very dreamlike and transparent . . . has now become a real thing in a printing press, and it's going through a big machine, and it looks lousy, and it has to be done again. And so gradually your particular transparent little dream is becoming more real, and more terrible every moment. And then finally it is

a book. And you become extremely depressed, because you realise that [it] . . . is really just another book! How strange. . . . And then it goes out into the world, and your child, who was so private and who was living with you for two years, now is everybody's child. Some people knock him on the head, some kick him in the rump, and others like him very much. It's a totally different experience. (Sendak 1977: 253–4)

Publication doesn't depress everyone, but most writers seem to feel outside their finished words. We encourage students to keep intellectual journals at university because they often gain confidence in their abilities when they reread the ideas fixed in ink. Likewise, before setting writing aside, to lie fallow, I print a perfect copy. When I return to it, it feels uncannily foreign, giving me more confidence in my accomplishment or greater resolve in my rewriting.

Speech and writing have different relations to time. Because writing suspends the flow of time, so that the first word coexists with the last, it allows writers and readers to go backward or forward at will. Writers have a chance to produce a coherent line of thought, both by organising ideas into a set of steps leading to a destination, and by erasing ideas that might reveal the tensions and exclusions on which the linear effect relies. When the inkiness of writing is denied, the simplicity of the line appears not as a writer's achievement but as the inevitability of Truth made manifest.

By freeing readers from reliance on memory, writing also makes close readings possible. The written text is fixed in ways speech is not. Caught in a moment, it can be searched at length for a single, logical, non-contradictory meaning. It can be read for the letter of the law, which is clear, objective and precise because it is (allegedly) filtered through the single sense of sight.

Writing's temporality, line and abstraction, then, may be crucial to the generation of the concept of abstract thought. As Barthes argues, 'Wherever there is a concurrence of spoken and written words, to write means in a certain manner: *I think better*, more firmly; I think less for you, I think more for the "truth"' (1991: 6).

* * *

This chapter has suggested that many qualities associated with sociological thought are actually qualities of writing. Sociology is to writing as the proper text of a sociology book is to the prelim pages. When aspiring to the condition of Knowledge per se, sociology pretends it can do without that on which it relies. Reliance must be denied, ink must become invisible, because it undermines the discipline's claim to transcend its specific social location.

Once fantasies of universal knowledges are discarded, recognition of sociology's traditional inkiness is no cause for embarrassment. Itself an affirmation of sociology's inspiring capacity to estrange the familiar, this recognition extends the discipline's capacities by challenging us to use writing and other media more honestly, knowingly and creatively.

Reading

One first needs a good desire to eat, drink and read. . . . Thus, in the morning, before the books piled high on my table, to the god of reading, I say my prayer of the devouring reader: 'Give us this day our daily hunger . . .' (Bachelard 1971: 26)

This quotation is irresistible. Around reading it brings together some of the central themes in this book. Reading needs a desire, an appetite, a hunger, a passion. Reading is like eating and drinking; it *is* an eating, drinking, devouring. Eating is an ordinary everyday activity. It is also ritualised and magical, and frequently has religious elements to it. And so it is with reading – an activity that is both everyday *and* magical and passionate. Potentially, at least.

Whilst I might value passionate moments in the ordinary, the everyday, and thus have an interest in the experience of reading in such terms, this is just one possible experience of reading. Reading has a certain meaning for Bachelard, through an association with eating; it will have different meanings for others. Reading a tax form, Bachelard, Ruth Rendell, *Fiabe italiane*, are different reading experiences, as too are reading on a train, at a desk, in bed. Reading means differently. This is the point that is most strikingly brought out in the Bachelard quotation. The metaphoric play with reading and eating jolts us into an awareness that there is no singular meaning or experience of reading. Put reading in relation to another activity, something other than eating, and it will mean differently.

One of the central claims of this book is that there is no non-metaphoric realm of fixed and natural meanings. Meaning is produced metaphorically, through a transfer between domains or terms, a transfer that in a way forces us to *make* sense. Language,

Merleau-Ponty says, is 'like a charade', 'understood only through the interaction of signs, each of which, taken separately, is equivocal or banal' (1964: 42). We are never speaking or thinking about one thing or sign alone, but always about terms in relation to each other. Eating and reading, for example, or language and a charade.

If language is a charade and words are 'dogged by incredible linguistic hazards' (Merleau-Ponty 1962: 188), then reading, in the sense of what one makes of the meaning of any particular text, becomes problematic. The very term 'reading' in contemporary cultural theory has come to the fore as a means of putting into question the notion of a singular meaning–reading of a text. Thus reading has displaced notions such as interpretation which imply that there is *a* meaning to be found, if only one digs deep enough. If, however, there is no meaning waiting to be deciphered, no pure meaning, then how we read matters: practices of reading make a difference to the meaning. In this view reading is productive of meaning rather than a translation. And to recognise the constitutive character of reading is to open up creative possibilities in reading practices. This is the central concern of this chapter.

To pursue the significance of ways of reading for a moment, let me develop the eating metaphor. Eating is never just eating; there are ways and ways of eating, so that, for example, what might even seem to be the same food will mean differently depending on the social relations, social space, rituals and so on. In *School* we made reference to the ritual re-enactment of the powerful myth of eating the father, the primal feast. Such an eating is pervasive in academic practices of reading: an assimilation of the founding fathers of the discipline. These reading practices assume a singularity in reading, that the meaning of a text is fixed, by the Father–Author. And in making this assumption, they deny their own eating, and 'cooking' through digestion. In claiming to translate the word, they refuse to acknowledge that their mastery of the Fathers is just that – a (passive) aggressive consumption which dominates and makes the text over in the reader's image. The important critical point here is the failure of reflexivity on the part of these practices, the denial of *reading*.

The form of reading we are proposing would also unsettle the notion of reading as a passive consumption to the active production of writing–cooking (Calvino 1993: 124–5; de Certeau 1984: xxi). One of the central themes in this chapter is that of activity, or, more precisely, a way of thinking about reading that disrupts an active–passive distinction. Not simply a consumption of a pregiven meaning, reading is both an eating and a cooking. The sort of reading that I am advocating here would be attentive to the nuances of a text: neither passive nor active, it would listen to a text, even as it transformed that text (Cixous 1988: 148).

If reading is not simply an eating, writing might not be simply a cooking either, but a form of eating, a nourishment (Derrida 1978: 231). I sometimes feel hungry for writing. One way or another the experience of writing can be very oral: think of the need that people have to eat, chew, drink or smoke while they write. (And once on this train of thought, writing can also be associated with anality, excrement, throwing up, giving birth . . .) The contemporary concern with reading as a site of meaning processes is encapsulated in the notion of reading as a writing. Barthes, for example, is concerned with closing the gap between writing and reading, with reading practices that open texts out, 'set them going' (Barthes 1977: 163): with (active–passive) practices that might be described as reading–writing or writing–reading.

For Barthes and Bachelard a reading that is closely connected with writing is a passionate reading. For Barthes this is a 'desiring reading' (1986: 39–41). Bachelard speaks of a 'joy' in reading that prompts a joy in writing, a desire to participate in the creative process (1969: xxii). Our principal concern is to introduce students to ways of reading which not only offer them an active part, but which also prompt them to write, to create. Our hope, quite simply, is that reading will be a joy and that we can introduce ways of reading that will have this effect (while not denying the effects of different sorts of texts, contexts and reading experiences). Indeed we hope that reading this book will be a pleasure and that it will invite you to write. It is with precisely this aim in mind that we have decided to talk about academic practices and mediations, making the assumption that a development of a competency and a reflexivity with respect to these is likely to enhance pleasure and prompt a creative desire.

This notion of *reading* parallels the understanding of *writing* introduced previously. It is through an awareness of itself as reading that *reading* becomes a form of writing. And, as we will see, the claim that reading is a writing brings the issue of the self to the fore. Where is the self in the reading process? What self is this? How does the self figure in meaning processes? If this sounds like a philosophical question, it is also thoroughly practical: what am I doing when I read?

* * *

In two famous essays – 'From Work to Text' and 'The Death of the Author' – Barthes sets out the central ideas that have come to inform contemporary understandings of reading. These revolve around the substitution of text for work and the displacement of the author by the reader–writer. The very displacement of the Author/God/Father, owner of the work, closes the distance between reading and writing. The text and the reader involve assumptions about meaning or signification processes that challenge those associated with work and author. To put it simply, what is called into question is the idea of *a* meaning or a signified, an ultimate meaning, a truth.

> Once the Author is removed, the claim to decipher a text becomes quite futile. To give a text an Author is to impose a limit on that text, to furnish it with a final signified, to close the writing. (Barthes 1977: 147)

The issue here is the authority of the modern figure of the Author, or more precisely the authority of those who would impart the intentions of the Author. In the Author resides an explanation of a work; interpretation is the activity of identifying this explanation, reducing a work to an author (Bachelard 1971: 8–9). All of which is to assume 'an explanation', and privilege it as a form of knowledge. It is also to make certain assumptions about the writing subject: the author who is the origin and ground for truth of the work is a self that is 'given' and expressed in writing. But what is really at stake is the status of the interpreting subject and the authority that is attached to possession of authorial intention – speaking in the name of the Father. To remove the Author is to challenge paternal power vested in the interpreting subject, it is to refuse to fix meaning and to open texts to a multiplicity in meaning, displacing meaning itself *and* empowering the reader. Reading is a process of meaning or signification, a process in which a text is transformed, not simply read but rewritten. As Barthes suggests, *reading* keeps the writing open.

This has enormous implications for the teaching relation. Imagine the possibilities that open up if, in learning, the student engages in a practice of *reading*. I am suggesting that there is a tension around or struggle between teacher as reader and student as reader and that this is about *different* reader positions and different forms of reading. For example, constituting certain theorists as founding fathers involves both reading them in a particular way, interpreting works in terms of intentions, *and* positioning oneself as the son, heir, interpreter. The authority of the teacher is established through a particular way of reading, which is a denial of *reading* and, indeed, through its insistence on singularity, a denial of the feminine.

This is most apparent in courses with titles like 'classical sociology' where students are told that there is a core – a norm – to the discipline in the works of the founding fathers and that the students' starting point must be to grasp the intentions of the Fathers. The lecturers – together with a judicious selection of secondary texts – will provide the interpretation of works: 'this is what Marx means'. Students must pay their respects to the Fathers before entering the family of Sociology. 'You must get this right before you can have your own thoughts about anything, certainly something as sacred as Marx or Weber.' The textbook is another example of this, providing accounts of *the* meaning of Marx, Weber, Durkheim. It commonly consists of oversimplified, predigested exegeses of primary texts which discourage students from reading these texts, from getting near to them, let alone engaging in a close reading of them. After this (spoon-)feeding experience, students frequently become dependent on textbooks, fearing an encounter with a primary text. Students are positioned as passive receivers, disempowered. They are invited neither to *read* Marx, Weber, Durkheim, nor to put them to use in relation to their own social worlds. If they did, the authority and power of the teacher/priest/interpreter of the 'Word of God' might be challenged.

Drawing a comparison between the control of the text by the teacher and the power of the Church, de Certeau says that 'a frontier' is set up 'between the text and its readers' by 'official interpreters who transform their own reading . . . into an orthodox "literality"' (1984: 171). The very idea of a 'literal meaning' is, then, he suggests, an 'index of social power'. A plurality of readings emerges with the decline in power of the institution, or those controlling the text, allowing readers/laypeople/students to come into contact with the text. Creative reading on the part of students thus presents a potential threat to the authority of the teacher and the discipline (de Certeau 1984: 172).

Closely associated with the notion of a singular or literal meaning is the idea of a unified work. The Author is a unifying presence. A good deal of interpreting work is concerned with ironing out apparent contradictions, making a work coherent, producing it as such. Divergences between texts, for example, will be accounted for in terms of the life-story, the progress from the young Marx to the old Marx. Why is unity to a work so important? (One of the key questions asked of an author not yet established as an Author is: is the work consistent and coherent?) Perhaps what is at issue here is the unity of the interpreting subject. A unified, coherent author implies a unified, coherent reader – a singularity in meaning, a singularity in the subject. The notion of the multiplicity in and dispersion of meaning has profound implications for an understanding of the reading subject. Once the Author is removed, so too is a coherent, originary reader: the mirror. The reader is constituted in the relation of reading. The reading self might be produced as contradictory, wandering (Barthes 1977: 159) or as fixed, but whatever the specific nature of this self might be, it is constituted in that relation with the text. It is the reading practices themselves which are productive of either a fixity or a movement in the self.

Issues about the self and reading immediately raise questions about objectivity and subjectivity in reading. Identifying a final or literal meaning is tied to the notion of being objective, a value central to the self-representation of sociology as a science. Literal truth is said to be located in a source external to the text, either in an Author or in 'social reality' (the text being an expression of either of these). The objective social scientist is also outside the text. With objectivity, then, textuality and mediations disappear, including the mediations of the reading social scientist. To suggest that the reader is 'in the text', or connected with that which is being read, does not amount to saying that readings are merely subjective. As we will see, what is at issue is a refiguring of the relation between text and reading subject in a way that displaces the objective–subjective distinction, a distinction which curiously denies the cultural.

'The text' itself unsettles a notion of an outside, or a source, an originary moment. A text is a weave, a tissue, a network of traces of other texts, other cultural products; 'woven entirely with citations, references, echoes, cultural languages . . . which cut across it through and through in a vast stereophony' (Barthes 1977: 160). Whether we are talking about a written text or some other cultural product, the point is that a text is never complete unto itself, a unified identity, and nor is it the expression of an outside source. Any source is itself woven. Thus the scientific grounds for truth are themselves culturally produced, they are 'inside the text' so to speak. And the very process of reading contributes to the weave: a cultural language is brought to the text (and subjectivity must itself be a cultural language), the context is a thread in the text. And it is also for this reason that however much a text or a reading claims closure, texts are always potentially open, without end.

Now let me return to the student as *reader* of texts of Marx, Weber and Durkheim. What is involved in *reading* such texts? (Not only these texts of course. But one of the issues here is the way in which these texts are regarded as sacred and read in a way that marks them off from others, treated as closed books.) In the first place *reading* implies that the texts themselves be read (translations actually, for English speakers, which raises issues that should be taken seriously), that students directly engage with primary texts, rather than accept secondary interpretations claiming to be direct representations. Once it is no longer a matter of 'Which is the real Marx?' the reader is free to put the text to work, to actively engage with the text and explore its possibilities. This active engagement comes of a very close reading that is neither slavish nor dominating, a close reading *relation* in which the text is brought to life.

There are all sorts of ways in which we can put a text to work.

One very productive strategy is to read texts against and with each other. This might involve a dialogue between theoretical texts or between a theoretical text and a social text or one's own experience or story. In this sort of reading strategy the interpretative, hermeneutic question 'What is the meaning of this or that?' is displaced. And neither is a theoretical text employed to provide a model or an explanation of a social text. The question becomes: how are *both* texts transformed in the process? This is a creative activity that works like metaphor (see *Magic*) – a text, the weave, is produced through the transformation of other texts.

A text can also be put to work against and in relation to itself. (In *Knowing* we will discuss this reading strategy with specific reference to Durkheim.) An internal reading of a text is based on the same assumptions as an inter-textual reading – that indeed any text is already inter-textual and not hermetically sealed off; a text is multiple, internally divided or in a relation with itself, if you like. The idea that a text is contradictory is thought of as something potentially positive rather than being regarded as cause for concern, grounds for dismissal, as itself providing creative opportunities. (Which is not to suggest that in writing we give up attempts at coherence, but, rather, that in living this desire we also recognise its impossibility.) One of the most important things about this approach to reading is that, where much academic reading looks for opportunities to reject as inadequate and faulty, it encourages a generosity in reading. Instead of looking for the fatal flaw (essentialism, idealism . . .), *readers* look for the possibilities opened up by a text, which in turn puts more responsibility on them, readers, to make something of a text.

Whether or not it is acknowledged, any reading of a text will be constitutive. It will involve the reading of a text in relation to other texts, it will take place in a context, and it will involve a process of selection and organisation. A discovering of Marx is a creating of Marx. There is no one Marx, no true Marx. Reflect for a moment on the experience of reading–rereading a book. Is it ever the same book? As Calvino says of this experience: 'whether we use the verb "read" or the verb "reread" is of little importance' (1989: 127). In a sense every rereading is a first reading: books change, and we change. The rather simple point is this: we always see something different in a text depending on what else we are reading, in the light of different experiences, in the light of changes in ourselves and the questions we ask. When I look at my underlining of Chapter 1 of *Capital*, I am reminded that I have read this piece of Marx in at least three different ways; in terms of the capitalist mode of production, the operations of ideology and the semiotics of commodities. Is there a correct way? But it is not simply that there are different possible meanings to – interpretations of – a text. Rather, in the process of reading, meaning is being produced: I cannot help but read Marx from a position of the now, in relation to my current reading, in the context of a community of readers, scholars. Very different Marxes have been produced, and were produced, even when *he* was reading his work. If sociology is to live, texts such as those written by Marx need to be seen as open; if their meaning is fixed, what is there left to do with them?

In suggesting that it makes a difference if the constitutive nature of reading is acknowledged, I am not proposing a reflexivity just as a means of avoiding bad faith, however important this might be. What is of rather more significance is that taking up the position of *reader* will make a difference to how we read and the writing–reading that emerges. Elsewhere we have made similar points about writing and storytelling. If we recognise that we are telling stories, the potential of storytelling can be explored. If we recognise that we are *reading*, we will give up asking 'What did the author mean?' and ask instead 'How do I as reader understand this?' (Barthes 1986: 30). What does this text do for me? What are the possible ways into it, and through it? By putting myself in an active relation to the text, I open up imaginative possibilities: for example, of making creative combinations of texts, or putting unlikely texts into dialogue with each other. This also involves being open to the idea that every reading of a text is a new reading: 'When one allows himself to be animated by new images, he discovers iridescence in the images of old books' (Bachelard 1971: 25). Such reading practices bring texts to life. And, as Bachelard suggests, they animate the reader.

The reader has displaced the Author. This should not be taken to imply that the reader is a substitute end point to meaning. Reading might be thought of as listening–playing which unsettles a final location of meaning (Barthes 1977: 162; Cixous 1988: 148).

If there is any site of meaning, it is in the relation, the listening–playing relation, between text and reader.

* * *

> haven't you ever happened *to read while looking up from your book*?
> (Barthes 1986: 29)

This is how Barthes begins an essay called 'Writing Reading'. He
goes on to speak of 'that text which we write in our head *when we
look up*' (1986: 30). The book sets us on a train of thoughts, associations, memories, anticipations of meanings; we (day)dream; and
in that moment of reading–dreaming we are already writing. De
Certeau speaks of an active creative reading as a dancing with the
text:

> the drift across the page, the metamorphosis of the text effected by
> the wandering eyes of the reader, the improvisation and expectation
> of meanings inferred from a few words, leaps over written spaces in
> an ephemeral dance. (1984: xxi; see also 175)

The question that I want to address here is: How does the creative process of reading work? How does reading become a
writing? What are the connections between reading and the
workings of the imagination?

What are the conditions of possibility of a creativity in reading?
We all know very well that this is not what a lot of reading is like.
Hurriedly reading before a class, in the office, in the corridor, trying to work out what the hell is going on, 'what are the key points
in the reading?', is probably neither a pleasurable nor a creative
experience. And of course, the institution encourages this sort of
reading practice. Overwhelmed by the sheer quantity of reading
at university, students are often tempted by the solution of speed
reading, and feel impatient with texts like Bachelard that refuse to
yield up a point, demanding a slower, deeper reading. It is difficult to resist a commodified approach to reading when the
assumption that 'the more one reads, the more one knows' is so
pervasive. But other reading practices *are* possible, practices
which generate richer, more interesting and engaging readings.

To pursue the issue of creative reading – or writing reading – I want to turn to Bachelard's account of creative imagination. For Bachelard, creativity consists in the re*living* of an image in a 'manner that is new' (1969: xxix), it involves being receptive to the 'ecstasy of the newness of the image' (1969: xi). This suggests to me that a creative reading is a passionate reading.

Reverberation is the central idea in Bachelard's phenomenology of creative imagination: poetic images work by reverberating in the reader. (I take the poetic to be broadly defined here, associated with creativity.) When an image reverberates in us, we live that image, we experience the image. If an image reverberates, it moves us, emotionally and bodily – we feel it. The poetic image works by taking hold of us, possessing us; readers abandon themselves to the poetic image (1969: xviii–xix, xxiv). It sets off waves within the reading self and between the self and the image, waves of imagination (1969: 36). More precisely, reverberations work by setting off a process of memory and dreaming in the reader, a dream-reading which prompts the imagination.

Through reverberations, the poetic image becomes 'our own', it moves us in 'our depths'. 'It has been given us by another, but we begin to have the impression that we could have created it, that we should have created it' (1969: xix). Reverberating in us, the poetic image prompts further reverberations. The reader is transformed: 'the reverberations bring about a change of being'. The poetic image 'expresses us by making us what it expresses', we have 'the experience of emerging'; this is a becoming of our being (1969: xix, xxiii). If the image expresses us, the reading process is also a writing, a reverberation. In the joy of reading we participate in creation. The poetic image 'has a bracing effect on our lives' (1969: xxii): we are moved, to write.

A relation of reverberation between the image and the reader, or text and reader, displaces any notion of origin or source of *a* meaning in an author, in a text, or in a reader. Meaning happens in-between. Bachelard's way of putting this is to say that every reading is originary (1969: xx). Creativity comes of being open to this idea, experiencing the newness of an image in one's encounter with it. And through such an experience an image is brought to life again, differently.

This bringing to life occurs because of a quality in the image itself, it has to work its magic on us, through us. Some images and forms of writing work for us, others don't. Bachelard works for me – with every reading I re-experience the newness of 'the image' and am moved – but I don't presume that he necessarily has that effect on you. However, in Bachelard's account it is not only the quality of the text that matters where creativity is concerned, but the quality of the space of reading. Bachelard works for me, but not just anywhere; I will find it difficult to sustain a joy in reading if I am reading him in the corridor. In *The Poetics of Space* Bachelard claims that it is intimate space, physical–psychical spaces of well-being, that provide the possibility of creative imagination. Shelter and protection make dreaming and remembering possible – daydreaming and imagining (1969: 5–7). If this should seem too sheltered and inward looking, it might be noted that he also speaks of the creative effects of spaces of movement – roads, paths (1969: 10). But the point here is that the space of reading makes a difference to how we read, whether or not we 'read while looking up from our book'.

* * *

Where do you read? In bed, at a desk, in an armchair by the fire (the closed warmth of the inside, one of Bachelard's examples of intimate spaces of dream-reading), in the toilet, on the train, on the beach, in the library? Are these the same experiences? And what do you read in each of these different places? Even when we do read the same book, is it the *same*, or in what sense the same, in bed, at the desk, on the beach, in the library?

I, for example, cannot read on a train; this is time for dreaming without a book. My feeling is always: what a wasted opportunity to have one's nose in a book; trains provide such good dreaming conditions, the movement, the gaze through the window. The pleasure of dreaming on trains can outweigh the pleasure of reading, although I realize that for many it is a space of shelter and regression, ideal for reading (see de Certeau 1984). I wonder then if this train-dreaming might not be thought of as a reading, a version of dream-reading? And having written this I now find a passage in Bachelard on precisely this experience of train trips (1969: 62).

In an essay called 'On Reading' Barthes attempts a classification of reading experiences in which the space of reading is central. On the library, which doesn't work for him, Barthes says:

this is a space visited, not inhabited, a site of repression. And yet, for many, the library is heaven, the epitome of a scholarly way of being.

Barthes speaks of the responsibility and irresponsibility of the table and the bed respectively (1991: 181). He says that the classification of books as 'bed' and 'table' is a means of controlling a certain frenzy of reading that occurs once writing has begun, when everything one reads finds its way into the work (1991: 181). I recognise Barthes's strategy and presume it is a common one. But where he suggests that this is a simple solution, it doesn't altogether work in my experience. Despite differentiations, what I read in bed often ends up in the writing; the book might have to be moved to the desk; I might have to get out of bed to make a note to myself. This has just happened to me. I wanted a break, in the afternoon, from writing, so, on the bed, I started to read Malouf's *Remembering Babylon*. I had been writing about Bachelard on the living of images. In Malouf, I found it. A description, that is, of the living of images in children's fantasy and play:

> the paddock, all clay-packed stones and ant trails, was a forest in Russia – they were hunters on the track of wolves. The boy had elaborated this scrap of make-believe out of a story in the fourth grade Reader; he was lost in it. Cold air burned his nostrils, snow squeaked underfoot; the gun he carried, a good sized stick, hung heavy on his arm. (1993: 1)

Children in a hot Australian paddock which *is* a forest in icy Russia – a lovely description of the enactment of metaphor. But what works in this image is Malouf's imaginings of the children's imaginings, such that we find ourselves in the place of children, hunters in the paddock–forest. Such writing prompts us into imaginative enactment. Well this reader anyway. This is what I take the living of images in Bachelard's work to be about. And thus this book was transported from the bed to the desk.

In general terms Barthes is right about the distinction between bed and desk; they do have very different associations. And as spaces of reading they produce different selves. Think, for example, of the imaginary of the relation with the book when reading in bed, the regression, on the one hand, and, on the other, the rather fearful side of the symbolic order of the desk, say before a lecture or tutorial (when one hides under the bedclothes till the last moment). But the desk can be a site of pleasure too, and intellectual passion. I am unlikely to feel, or at least sustain, a passion for knowledge while reading in bed; when a book in bed prompts intellectual passion, I must get up, to my desk. And this doesn't feel like 'responsibility' exactly either. So, different reading spaces produce different experiences and meanings of reading, but, of course, the text, context and purpose of reading make a difference too.

> You are about to begin reading Italo Calvino's *If on a winter's night a traveler*. Relax. Concentrate. Dispel every other thought. Let the world around you fade. Best to close the door; the TV is always on in the next room. . . . Find the most comfortable position: seated, stretched out, curled up, or lying flat. Flat on your back, on your side, on your stomach. In an easy chair, on the sofa, in the rocker, the deck chair. . . . On top of your bed, of course, or in your bed (Calvino 1982: 9)

What is most memorable about the opening to *If on a Winter's Night a Traveler* is the detailed description of getting the right position for reading, positioning the body for reading. Another way of thinking about different reading experiences and practices would be to put it in terms of different reading bodies. Reading Malouf while lying in bed *feels* different from reading Malouf while sitting up at the desk. In each case a different reading body is involved.

*　＊　＊*

> Reading is the gesture of the body (for of course one reads with one's body). (Barthes 1986: 36)

Of course? The notion that we read with our body, I find, is greeted not merely with surprise, but with shock. A shock that, in part, comes of recognition. Yes, I can feel it in the throat, stomach, shoulders; my hands, head, feet are moving; I am speaking, to myself. 'Now you mention it, it seems so obvious, but I would never have thought that my *body* was reading a book.' Why is the recognition that we read with our bodies so shocking? There seems to be something transgressive about this. Is it because what is supposedly cerebral turns out to be sensual, even erotic, potentially? The cerebral as the mark of repression, the repression of *reading*?

Comparing this disembodied reading experience with plane travel, de Certeau claims that it is a particularly modern experience of reading associated with the privileging of the eye:

> Today, the text no longer imposes its own rhythm on the subject, it no longer manifests itself through the reader's voice. (1984: 176)

The shift from the voice to the eye allows for a relation of distance between text and reader and invites a bodily experience that feels disembodied. The trees and rivers of the text (Cixous 1988: 148) are no closer than those of the country over which we fly.

In contrast to this type of reading, writers such as Barthes and Cixous are interested in reading practices that involve a close relation with the text. Claiming that there is a bodily relation between text and reader, Cixous says: 'We work . . . as close to the body of the text as possible' (1988: 148). Barthes wants an eroticism of reading, a 'desiring reading' in which 'all the body's emotions are present' (1986: 39). Think of *The Pleasure of the Text* and Barthes's concern with the materiality, the erotic of textual practices of writing and reading: the bliss or *jouissance* of the text.

Cixous chooses to work on texts which 'touch' her, texts which she 'loves'; Barthes looks for texts of disturbing pleasure; Bachelard values poetic writing which sets off joyous reverberations. Texts invite different bodily–emotional responses. Some leave us cold, some make us feel sick, others voracious, turned on, high, joyful or sad. A text can set up rhythms in us, set us singing, set us dancing. A text *can* move us, despite the repressions of contemporary reading, particularly duty reading (de Certeau 1984: 175). And the effect of a text on the body can tell us something about how the text's signs work; if we listen, that is. I suggest to students that they begin an analysis or reading of a text – any text, written or otherwise – by asking: what effect does this have on my body? This question is itself strategic in a shift from repression to desire. And I find it works, despite the initial resistance along the lines of 'Why does my response matter?' By paying attention to our responses we can get a sense of how

meaning is produced, how a text means, in terms of: the semantic content, the formal relations between elements, and the nature
of the signifying system (a visual text is going to have a different
effect from a piece of music). We respond to cultural codes of
signs; every reading 'derives from trans-individual forms'
(Barthes 1986: 31), even if it is also particular.

If we think of reading as a living, dynamic relation between
text and reader, then it is clear that not everyone will have the
same response to any particular text. Indeed such a notion would
seem as strange as the idea that we would all fall in love with the
same person. Here we are touching on one of the central themes
of this book, namely that of mediations: the mediations of the
body, and emotions, in reading. In the inter-subjective relation of
love something is undoubtedly going on, emotionally, bodily;
there is no simple transmission of love as if it were some thing
separate from the relation. And so it is with relations of reading.
In the reading process meaning is being *produced*, sensually, ma-
terially; meaning, *a* meaning, is not being transmitted–received
directly. And it is not as if the body passively absorbs meaning,
like a sponge; a physical–emotional response to a text implies an
active relation. Barthes says 'to read is to make our *body* work . . .
at the invitation of the text's signs' (1986: 31). This resonates with
Derrida's formulation: 'we are written only as we write'. But
Barthes takes this further by specifying that it is the body which
writes: our body works, our body reads; our body is a site of signification processes.

* * *

Whether it is a question of newspapers or Proust, the text has a meaning only through its readers (de Certeau 1984: 170)

In reading texts, we bring our knowledge of the world to them,
and we bring our lives to them – our bodies, our memories, our
dreams. The particularity of our stories and experiences is implicated in the reading. As a consequence of our different histories,
our cultural knowledges, we tune in to different moments of the
text and pick up on different meanings. But it is not simply that
there are multiple meanings there in the text, waiting to be seen
by different reading subjects. The self is implicated in the very

production of meaning of the text, the self becomes part of the textual weave in the reading process. Cultural traces in the text mix with our memory traces in a reading which is both cultural and particular.

What seems curious to me is the denial of the reading subject in the name of objectivity. How is reading *experienced* by those who would hold with notions of an objective reading and the text as an object, distinct from a reading subject? Reading itself must be repressed in an objective reading. What sort of experience is that of a disembodied consciousness that sees clearly the meaning of a text, that does not engage with a text? For surely in any engagement the text will be contaminated with the self, a relationship will be established between the text and self.

To acknowledge that the reading self is in the text is to question the idea of an objective reading. But does that make reading a merely subjective matter? The contentious issue about subjectivity and reading is this: with the death of the Author and the questioning of a fixity of meaning are we left with the implication that texts can mean anything you like? Although such notions are sometimes attributed to Barthes, he questions the idea of a 'wild reading', claiming that reading 'needs structure, it respects structure' even if it *'perverts* structure' (1986: 36). He calls into question a shift from 'polysemy to the point of asemy', the liberating of reading from all meaning except *'my* reading' (1986: 324). The general structuralist–semiotic point here, and it is one taken as given by post-structuralists, is that meaning is produced through structurally determinate relations between signs; there *are* rules.

> [in] reading, we too imprint on the text a certain posture, and it is for this reason that it is alive; but this posture, which is our invention, is possible only because there is a governed relation among the elements of the text. (Barthes 1986: 32)

The rules, the governed relation among elements, make possible the transformations in relations between elements in reading – our inventions. When we falter, and read a sentence over again, playing with the different possible inflections, different intonations, we are weighing up the rules or codes, both intra-textual and inter-textual, and thinking 'What do these make possible?' Drawing on a metaphor from Borges, Eco says 'a wood is a garden of forking paths . . . the reader is forced to make choices all the time' (1994: 6). Choices in reading presuppose certain 'world knowledges' on the part of the reader. Eco constantly emphasises the necessity of the reader's competency with respect to cultural conventions (1992, 1994); any old reading will not do. But it is precisely a reading competence that allows for a creativity in reading. With every *close* reading we read a text differently.

Another way of putting this – possibly more in tune with Barthes than Eco – might be to say that order and disturbance go together, that it is this combination that constitutes the transformation of meaning. The formulation 'order and disturbance' displaces the objective–subjective distinction insofar as the latter assumes an extra-textual ground of truth. As Barthes puts it: 'there is no objective or subjective truth of reading' (1986: 31). His claim that there is only a *'ludic* truth' suggests that we think of truth as thoroughly cultural and contingent, located in that living relation between reader and text, in the play–work, performance, of *reading*.

The idea that order and disturbance or structure and movement go together is similar to the point made about dressage in *Writing*: the discipline of dressage facilitates freedom of movement, it 'allows'. A basic assumption, in this book and in our teaching, is that if students are provided with a structure – our courses are highly structured – and made aware of the rituals and rules of academic discourse, they are going to be in a better position to engage in creative activity. Needless to say, this includes challenging us: our courses are structured, but we do not make presumptions about where or how they will go, which paths will be taken. If this learning–teaching activity is in a sense 'subjective', it is also rigorous – you have to know the rules of the game to play. Indeed, in order to challenge a particular discipline and reading community, it is essential to be able to articulate the rules and conventions of the game.

Barthes says that he will 'abide by a particular reading (as any reading is?)' (1986: 33). But the particular does not amount to 'wild' or outside culture and sociality. Bachelard's phenomenological reading practice also privileges the particular: phenomenology considers 'the onset of an image in an individual consciousness' (1969: xv). We start with our experience of an image, for where else would one start? But in doing so we get at something of the trans-subjective of the image. The response 'I should have written that' expresses the pleasure of connection, sociality. And 'that rings true for me': my experience is particular, but I am not alone in having it. For an image to reverberate it must successfully combine the trans-subjective *and* the particular (in the manner of a Durkheimian experience of ritual). If the particular is not spoken to, if there is no reverberation in us, we are merely left with the general, an abstraction that is unlikely to move.

In Bachelard's account of reading, the movement of reverberation is the site of signification. Reverberation connects a reader and an image, it undoes a distinction between subject and object: 'the duality of subject and object is iridescent, shimmering, unceasingly active in its inversions' (1969: xv). Indeed if an image is to reverberate in us it cannot be treated as an object, distinct and separate from a reading subject. Again we might say that meaning resides in neither the text nor the reader but in the in-between of the relation between reader and text.

* * *

A different world (the reader's) slips into the author's place.
     This mutation makes the text habitable, like a rented apartment. It transforms another person's property into space borrowed for a moment by a transient. (de Certeau 1984: xxi)

I began this chapter with a metaphoric play between reading and eating. Now I want to return to such transfers between everyday practices and reading.

The text is like a rented apartment, the reader a renter, making the text habitable. And thus de Certeau makes reading an everyday activity. One of his principal concerns is with the creative nature of practices of everyday life. He speaks of everyday arts, 'ways of making', 'poetic ways of making do' in practices of talking, reading, moving about, shopping, cooking, dwelling, walking in the street (1984: xiv–xxii). There is a potential for creativity in everyday practices; they are linguistic phenomena, like speaking, reading, writing. No sooner has the text been compared to a rented apartment than renters are compared to speakers: renters 'furnish' apartments with their acts and memories just as speakers bring their history and 'turns of phrase' to a language, 'as do pedestrians, in the streets they fill with the forests of their desires' (1984: xxi).

It is now quite commonplace to speak of everyday practices in terms of reading: we read a street, an apartment, a supermarket, an advertisement. What is the significance of this metaphor? The implication that social reality is textual is of rather less interest, it seems to me, than the emphasis on the *reading* of social texts. And this is what interests de Certeau: everyday life is creative because it involves the *practice* of texts. In terms of Saussurean semiotics he places emphasis on *parole* or the speech act rather than *langue* or the structure of the language (1984: xiii, 32–3). Any speech act presupposes a linguistic system, but a linguistic system is *realised* only through a speech act (1984: 32–3). *Langue* and *parole*, rather than constituting an opposition, are dependent upon each other. A text is actualised in the practice, or the *parole*, of reading (1984: 171). And if a system or a text is real only in the practice, this opens the way to creativity. Thus, in the supermarket, the kitchen and the street, we arrange and rearrange elements in what might be understood as an appropriation of languages. Just as we write when we read.

Reading–writing is a metaphor for everyday practice; it is also a metaphor for cultural analysis of such practice. We read the beach, a show on TV, a room. Thus cultural analysis is an everyday practice, it partakes of that which it would know. We also read Marx, Weber, Durkheim, Bachelard, de Certeau. Without denying the very different knowledges and skills required for reading different sorts of texts, might not the reading metaphor be strategic in making trouble for the sociological distinction between the theoretical and the empirical? And indeed for the privileging of a domain of practice marked out as knowledge over the everyday?

* * *

In an essay on the country of his childhood, 'The Light of the Sud-Ouest', Barthes makes a distinction between embodied and abstracted reading. He speaks of reading a place, of knowing the social composition of a place, through memories of sensations, sounds, light, but particularly smell. The 'coarse filter' of 'socio-logical analysis' 'loses the "subtleties" of the social dialect'. But he *felt* them. Memory, emotions, the senses, are all at work in his reading.

> For 'to read' a country is first of all to perceive it in terms of the body and of memory, in terms of the body's memory. I believe it is to this vestibule of knowledge and of analysis that the writer is assigned. (Barthes 1992: 8–9)

Reading a country will not be the same experience as reading a book; different senses and memories of sensations will be called upon. But Barthes is using reading here as a metaphor for know-ing, he is talking about the quality of our encounter with our world. And this encounter, this reading, is passionate.

Desire

For, unfortunately, Hegel isn't inventing things. What I mean is that the dialectic, its syllogistic system, the subject's going out into the other in order to come back to itself, this entire process . . . is, in fact, what is commonly at work in our everyday banality. (Cixous 1986: 78)

Desire is a relation, an emotional dynamic between the self and an other. It is also fundamental to the workings and motivations of knowledge: knowledge consists of a movement outside oneself into the world, a movement towards an other, whatever form that other might take, whether it be the otherness of another person, place, social world, or even the otherness inherent in an unfamiliar idea. Cixous is referring to Hegel's famous story of desire, the life and death struggle between the master and the slave, a story that has widely been taken as the model for desire in all social relations.

What Cixous is taking issue with is the particular nature of Hegelian desire, the structure of the self–other relation involved. Hegel assumes not just that all knowledge is self-knowledge and that knowledge is motivated by a desire to know ourselves, but that knowledge is about a desire to know a self that would stand alone in self-certainty. This is a solipsistic moment when supposedly I can say 'I' and believe that to be something entirely distanced and separated from that which is you – other. We might leave ourselves and move towards an other, but only with the desire to return to a self intact, a self more sure of itself for its contact with the other.

The Hegelian scenario of desire goes something like this: I desire the recognition of an other, I need the other to act as a mirror; but if you are to be my mirror you must be the same as me, any difference would threaten my identity (Hegel 1977: 112–15).

Imagine a lecture. Nods of the listeners' heads make lecturers feel confirmed in what they are saying and more certain of a sense of self. An audience is absolutely necessary for this; after all, if you weren't nodding back at me how could I be sure of myself? Then, unexpectedly, a student speaks out, questioning something I have just said; I falter, I am no longer alone, speaking, sure of my identity. An other has threatened my sense of self. Who will speak, me or them? And thus we have the beginnings of a life and death struggle. It is the desire for self-sameness and identity that makes a life and death struggle inevitable in this story. For this desire involves a negative, destructive relation to the other: the denial of any difference from the self in the other and the desire to destroy any specificity of the other. By contrast, Cixous has a vision of a desire that is life-giving; her concern is with the possibility of a desire which 'would keep the *other* alive and different' (1986: 79).

Hegelian desire is paradoxical: I need the other for recognition of self, there is no self without an other, yet self-certainty necessitates the negation of the other, otherness. In terms of knowledge, this irony could be put like this: the desire is for mastery and a finality to knowledge, a desire for a self that would stand alone in its self-knowledge; but this would bring desire, the very condition of knowledge, to an end. With no other and no desire there is no movement towards, that is, no process of knowledge. Ultimately, then, mastery fails. And thus Hegel's story undoes itself. (Self-)knowledge is social, it is constituted in a structure of mediation. Yet the desire is for a knowledge without mediation, outside social relations: an impossible but, as Cixous implies, very real fantasy. This book's concern with mediations of knowledge, and with sociology's denial of the mediations on which it is dependent – the denial of its own social character, in short – is framed implicitly by this Hegelian irony.

Different social relations of desire imply different forms of knowledge or ways of knowing. In a way the deconstructive turn in Hegel invites us to ask critical questions about the nature of the self–other relation in his story, and thus the possibility of different forms of relations and ways of knowing. For writers such as Cixous, the double moment of both the desire for mastery *and* the impossibility of the satisfaction of this desire opens up a space for other desires, desires which acknowledge *desire* – the relational of knowledge. Cixous constantly asks: what about the possibility of a movement towards the other with no need to overcome or negate, that is, destroy; a desire in which the other, and the otherness of the *relation between* is not only acknowledged but welcomed? It is precisely this relation which points to the impossibility of an absolute knowledge, a knowledge in possession of itself.

'[T]he dialectic . . . is . . . at work in our everyday banality.' While there are all sorts of issues about knowledge that might be addressed in connection with Hegelian desire, in this chapter I want to focus on the everyday of teaching. The fact that teaching exemplifies the *social* nature of knowledge accounts, perhaps, for the disdain that many academics have for it: teaching must be repressed by any knowledge that would deny its social character. My interest here is in the effects of such a desire in knowledge on the experience of the social relations of teaching; the connections between desire in knowledge and desire in teaching. My hope is that drawing attention to the social relations of teaching – that which would be repressed – might in itself open up the possibility of other forms of relations. If Hegel is at work, so too are other desires in teaching, here, now.

* * *

The communication model of teaching assumes that knowledge is something that might be possessed. It is some *thing* in the possession of the teacher, something which is to be transmitted or communicated to the student without any loss to the teacher, without any loss in self-possession. We have said a lot about these teaching practices, how the fantasy of hanging onto knowledge requires a denial that anything happens with knowledge in the teaching process. I sense something very Hegelian in all of this. And it's the air of tension and struggle as much as the structure of relations that gives an Hegelian feel. Perhaps I'm thinking of the struggle to maintain a particular structure and, with it, certain fantasies about a stability in knowledge.

The contested, contingent nature of knowledge is possibly nowhere more present than in the classroom. Thus the communication model is constantly being undermined: students *do* respond, they ask questions, they ask awkward questions, they don't speak, they adopt a blasé or bored attitude or one of *ressentiment*; one way or another they unsettle the teacher's self-certainty. Students remind us of the fragile basis of any certainty in knowledge, in self-knowledge. As Barthes puts it:

> I am the person who, under cover of *setting out* a body of knowledge, *puts out* a discourse, *never knowing how that discourse is being received* and thus for ever forbidden the reassurance of a definitive image . . . which would *constitute me*. (1977: 194)

Student responses need not be motivated by some alternative pedagogy to have an unsettling effect on the position of the teacher: 'I have done exactly what you told me to do, why have I not done better?' 'Your delivery of ideas has not been clear enough.' 'You are meant to have answers.' Furthermore, if I presume that students whom I teach will necessarily take up my views about the importance of student 'intellectual autonomy', I am operating within precisely the same Hegelian frame as the communication model, ironic as it might seem: 'Be as I wish you to be – be autonomous.' I shouldn't be surprised when students resist, get angry, take up a blasé attitude, but I too would seem to want the 'reassurance of a definitive image', a mirror. All of us, teachers and students, long for recognition, desire to be desired, even if we have no illusions about 'the truth of self-certainty'. So might we not seek recognition and simultaneously let go of a desire for self-certainty?

Teaching is a lived relation of knowledge. What is repressed in the communication model is very close to hand – an experience of knowledge which is embodied, affective, relational. In the presence of moving, speaking, silent, feeling bodies it is difficult to maintain notions of minds passively receiving pure ideas. Teaching is risky; the very process of imparting knowledge – if that is how teaching is understood – potentially threatens the self-assurance of the bearer of knowledge. Thus the *struggle* to negate. There is a lot at stake in the teacher-student power relation where a possessive knowledge is concerned.

* * *

The Hegelian structure of desire is oppositional. The full force of this emerges once we think of the *experience* as well as the formal structure of the teacher–student relation. The dialectic involves a power relation in which the dominant term denies dependency on the subordinate term: the fantasy of independence of teacher–academic requires a negation of student and a denial that the very term 'teacher' only exists in relation to 'student'. To reiterate a point made in *School*: in order that they might retain a fantasy of intellectual security, teachers produce students as 'a nightmare of intellectual insecurity'. And one suspects that a good deal of projection and punitive identification is involved here. Students are other – to be kept at a distance. We have earlier discussed some of the most visible manifestations of this in the physical organisation of space in lecture and tutorial rooms, but this spatiality is produced in more subtle forms as well, through the constitution of student 'intellectual insecurity' for instance. Distance is necessary to preserve the sacredness of the teacher, the purity of a knowledge in possession of itself, from the contaminating effects of students. This need for distance indicates something of the fragility of the position of intellectual security.

Distancing strategies involve a sort of negative mirroring – that is not me. This sort of negation of the other works on a principle of sameness since the other is constituted only with reference to the self: the same or not the same. Any qualitative difference or specificity is denied. There are other, apparently more positive forms of relations with students – relations characterised by closeness rather than distance – that are based, none the less, on the same structure of desire. The refusal to allow for difference in students is exemplified perhaps by the paternal–familial model of relations that we have spoken about. The previous account of the constitution of writers as fathers has obvious pedagogic implications: many teachers would take the place of the father. Talk about the need for heirs and progeny is common amongst academics (and regrets that 'students aren't as they used to be' – like me – is the other side to this). Moreover, a feminist pedagogy which would substitute the nurturing mother for the father does nothing to break with the family model in which students are positioned as children (Gallop 1994).

Only a few privileged students become part of the family, and to these students the father might be as nurturing as the mother.

The chosen few are admitted to the ranks on the condition that they act as mirror to the father–mother–teacher: 'you will be the same as me', 'the student I was or might have been'. This is projection of course, we see what we want to see in the mirror; identity means a refusal to see and hear the relation, for in relations things happen, terms change, the economy of sameness cannot be maintained. In the stifling, suffocating intensity of these kinds of familial relations the gap between self and other is completely closed. It might be more accurate to say that there is no gap allowed in the first place: here is a relation of the other to the self as mere extension, a relation that is not a relation, without differentiation or separation. This is an inversion of the distance model which amounts to the same: in both cases the passage between is erased, movement is suspended.

Is there something curious about the fact that this familial model, paternal or maternal, is most obvious in thesis supervision relations, precisely when intellectual independence might be expected? But then again perhaps that is precisely the point. The success of the student is the teacher's success, 'my bright baby'. Such relations tend to be exclusive, possessive and demanding of loyalty, the identity of the teacher becoming completely caught up in the academic achievements of the student (as an attempted resolution of disappointments in oneself?).

Whilst the authoritarian nature of these adult–child relations is quite apparent, denials that there are power relations between teachers and students can be just as authoritarian. I'm thinking of teaching approaches that are represented as non-authoritarian, such as handing it over to the class to decide what a course will be about: 'I haven't done a course outline, let's go down to the pub and talk about what you would like to do.' Supposedly a refusal of authority, such a position might well amount to an appropriation of the place of student, and, thus, another version of an Hegelian power relation. Denials of a power relation can thus have the effect of a denial of *differences* between teachers and students.

* * *

Disrupting an opposition is not to be taken as an erasure of difference. Quite the contrary. An opposition works on an either/or principle of sameness; terms are mutually exclusive. Disrupting a teacher–student opposition involves above all else a recognition of a transfer, a passage between two different terms, terms that have both a specificity and a dependency on each other. The terms might not be equal, the exchanges between them might not be equal, but to recognise that there are exchanges and that these have effects on each of the terms is to allow oneself to be open to change in the process of teaching, open indeed to changes in ways of knowing.

In the light of this dependency, the notion of student autonomy requires clarification, since one of my aims in teaching and in this book is to facilitate such autonomy. Rigorously speaking, student 'specificity' might be closer to what I have in mind than 'autonomy', given the associations of identity or self-presence with the latter. For I am not speaking about a reversal of substituting student independence for teacher independence. It's a matter of focusing less on the terms than on the relation, the 'being in relation' (Cixous 1992: 70), recognising the ways in which the relation is constitutive of the terms.

This involves acknowledging that the teacher–student relation is a power relation. Power relations are not simply erased. But power does not work in one direction. Nor indeed, does it work on an either/or model of possession and loss: 'either you have it or I do'. Again, by focusing on the relation it is possible to get a sense of the flows of power–knowledge, the passage between terms. For example, our observation exercise on 'power and ritual in the classroom' helps attune students to the materiality of knowledge rituals and the nuances of power in teaching, which in turn has the effect of shifting power relations, setting up a process of negotiation. The effects of these negotiations are in this text. Or to put this another way, this text has emerged, in part, in the context of shifting teacher–student power relations, and, I would say, the development of student 'autonomy'. The play of power has been productive for both teachers and students.

On the part of the teacher, the ideal of student autonomy requires a recognition of 'student', a recognition that I as teacher am constituted in this desiring relation, a relation that can bring to light my 'not knowing'. An acceptance of the other implies an acknowledgement that knowledge can never be final or complete, that knowledge *is* desire. It is the 'being-in relation' that generates pleasure and possibility in the experience of teaching–learning.

* * *

> The most difficult thing to do is to arrive at the most extreme proximity while guarding against the trap of projection, of identification. The other must remain in all its extreme strangeness within the greatest possible proximity. (Cixous 1988: 29)

Cixous's desire is that 'the other remains other' whilst ever so close. Unlike Hegelian desire this is a desire without opposition between self and other, without negation; it is a desire that values the passage between, the relation, a desire that values the strange. Whereas Hegelian desire involves a distance and sameness, this desire is structured around proximity and difference. (For me, this echoes Simmel's 'stranger' – one who combines proximity and distance [1950: 402].) This requires a real balance and lightness in a movement between the terms, 'an *in-betweenness* of two human beings, moving back and forth from one to the other' (Cixous 1992: 71). The stranger, Cixous says, is constantly under threat (1992: 70).

Cixous's vision of combining intimacy and distance, attachment and detachment, might be taken as an alternative model of teacher–student desire. This is a model to which I aspire, but one which I rarely achieve in practice; I don't as yet live it, embody it, being too caught up in the familial, albeit in a very ambivalent, contradictory way. But as Cixous says, we don't simply escape Hegelian desire and leap into some alternative, even if we do glimpse its possibilities. It might even be that Cixous's desire can only be experienced fleetingly. If we had it all the time, it would be something else – rather more Hegelian perhaps.

In practice, models of desire are combined in complex ways. So I shift between putting up protective barriers, keeping students at a distance, and being open to an engagement in which students' critical comments are part of the relation and not denied. I shift between allowing the occasional student who gets close to be different (or, perhaps allowing proximity because I value a difference in them), and wanting them to become like me. I find myself wanting students, particularly students such as these, to write as I would like to write. Does this mean that I would have them act as a mirror? Surely a desire for students to 'write well', to write as I would like to write, might also allow difference and acknowledge a difference without any envy.

This points to the difficulty of which Cixous speaks, of being close while avoiding projection and identification. And from the student side, the motivation to write for the teacher, the desire to be desired which can produce such good work, might not necessarily be based on a principle of sameness either: I wish to write for you and differently. Clearly, however, there is a very delicate balance in these sorts of relations: how to attain the closeness of support, admiration and recognition without grasping or wanting the same.

I would like to think that in our collaboration, Andrew and I have achieved this sort of balance. We write and teach differently. I admire and take pleasure in Andrew's writing and teaching, without a desire to be the same. But I acknowledge a tension around such a desire. When I *do* find myself tipping over into 'should I be more like him', I remind myself that I couldn't be, even if I tried, but, much more importantly, that Andrew values the way I write and teach. This mutual trust and respect makes difference possible: we write for each other, allowing the other to speak and to write. Difference works productively, without conflict, enabling both an excitement about ideas and a certain detachment.

The Cixousian model of desire comes of a concern to keep otherness alive, to retain the movement in the relation between self and other. In these terms teaching would be thought of as the teaching *relation* (rather than the transmission of some thing) and thus as a process without end. A recognition of the impossibility of an end to pedagogy, a strangeness in teaching itself, is potentially liberating for students and teachers. For this involves the recognition that knowledge is in the relation itself; it is not held or possessed by a knowing subject but produced in this relation. To be open to the other thus has profound implications for how we think about what we are doing in teaching, for how we think about knowledge. To paraphrase Cixous, the good teacher would be one who knows 'how not to possess what one knows' (1992: 67).

The model of near and far implies a transfer between terms, the student becoming teacher, the teacher becoming student. In *School* we talked about various ways in which the teacher is in a similar position to that of student, subjected to processes of examination and never arriving at a place of intellectual security. The other side to this is the student in the position of teacher. I shall say more about this in a moment, but, in very profound ways, it is from students that we learn what we know. When I speak about an exchange in the teaching relation, this is what I have in mind – a movement back and forth between these terms, teacher and student, a movement which subverts a demarcation line while retaining difference.

* * *

In a positive model of desire where otherness is recognised as the condition of knowledge, teaching is understood to be dialogic. 'No knowledge can be supported or transported by one alone' (Lacan, quoted in Felman 1982: 33). Without wishing to equate them, writers such as Barthes and Felman have found aspects of the psychoanalytic relation suggestive for thinking about the teaching relation. Freud and Lacan stress that analysis is an experience of knowledge that involves two subjects; and more than this, it is a listening–speaking exchange from unconscious to unconscious (Barthes 1985: 252–8; Felman 1982: 28–9). The knowledge in question needs the relation, it does not have an existence separate from the mediation of the teaching–learning relation. For Felman, the psychoanalytic implication is that the teacher cannot claim to be a self-possessed proprietor of knowledge; both intersubjectivity and the unconscious undo any illusion of a consciousness transparent to itself, self-presence. Dialogue in this view is far removed from a notion of the transmission of ready-made concepts. Rather it consists of a complex interaction between subjects who are never complete.

In Freud's pedagogy the teacher is one who recognises that learning has no end; 'the analysand is qualified to be an analyst as of the point at which he understands his own analysis to be inherently unfinished' (Felman 1982: 37). Thus the position of the teacher is the position of *'the one who learns'*, the one who *'teaches nothing other than the way he learns'*. The subject of teaching is 'interminably a student' (Felman 1982: 37). Felman is making this argument through a reading of Lacan and Freud. But it rings true for me, from my experience of teaching.

I find the idea that we teach the way we learn very exciting, and helpful, for thinking about what we are doing when we teach. It invites us to take up teaching approaches which demystify knowledge practices, for example by showing what we do: 'Here is how I would write a research proposal, write an essay, read a text; this is how I start writing a piece; this is what I do when I feel lost or stuck.' Of his place in the seminar Barthes says: 'I do not say what I know, I set forth what I am doing. . . . I am neither a sacred (consecrated) subject nor a buddy, only a manager, an operator, a regulator' (1986: 333). The difference between Barthes and other members of the seminar is that he has written. Thus, he suggests, as a means of eluding mastery, that he write in the presence of others, that he show a book *'in process'*: 'let us show ourselves *in the speech-act'* (1986: 339–40).

There is something liberating about being able to say to a tutorial: 'I don't know; but this is how I would begin to think about it, how I would set out the issues, pose questions.' This activity of working through an issue – thinking out loud – requires an engagement on the part of students, which is itself a skill that needs to be taught–learned. If this sort of thinking process is always intersubjective, it is most intense when the intersubjective relations are face-to-face. There is a risk involved in 'doing it on your feet' with others responding, listening, speaking, which, in turn, contributes to a sense of ideas in process. It is this sort of experience that confirms for me that we 'learn from students our own knowledge'. A tutorial, for example, has worked for me if it makes me think, if I go on thinking after the class. But my excitement about ideas is only made possible by students' excitement.

It might seem obvious to say that teaching and learning go together, but many academics would never say 'I don't know'. The position of student must be refused; for the dialogic implications of the teaching–learning connection are disturbing to a knowledge that longs for order, control and a truth of self-certainty.

* * *

Teaching is a desiring relation of speaking–listening. Speech is rather obviously the predominant medium or form of signification in teaching, and it is the one that we probably most associate with dialogue. But speech may or may not be dialogic. That depends on the desire. Elsewhere we have suggested that dialogic forms of writing are those which, by acknowledging the plurality of meaning, invite the reader to share in the creative process. To be open to the multiplicity of meaning is to be open to the other. So how might we specify this openness to the other in speech?

Speech is a signification form which particularly invites dialogue, and I believe that this is intimately connected with what Barthes describes as the polysemy of listening (1985: 258). There is something unstable, immediate, risky, corporeal about speech – the speech of teaching – that is profoundly unsettling to any fixity in meaning. A common response on the part of teachers is to attempt to control the speech of the classroom, to establish an oppositional set of relations between an active speaker and passive listeners. An alternative response would be to take pleasure in the risk of the intersubjectivity of a speaking–listening dialogue: pleasure in an active listening – a notion so well captured by Barthes's *'listening speaks'* (1985: 252, 259) – and a speaking that refuses the posturings of the master, that listens.

Writing this is prompting me to reflect on my own tendency to hierarchise writing and speech. I am very insistent that students 'write all the time'. There are institutional constraints which justify this. But beyond these, even if one values the creative form of writing, there is no reason for a hierarchisation: writing and speaking are both skills that need to be learned. I should listen to students who say they prefer to think through speaking rather than writing. They are *different* forms of thinking. And they can be put into play – speak to each other – in very productive, creative ways. Look at the number of times in this book when in speaking about one of these forms, we necessarily speak–write about the other. Here is another close relation, like that of reading–writing.

This is not to deny that there is a speaking in teaching that participates in the metaphysics of presence: the speech of the communication model of teaching, transmitting ideas with clarity and authority (Barthes 1977: 190–1). This is a speech that would abolish polysemy and deny its own corporeality. It doesn't work of course; even in a lecture, when we have the floor, we cannot control the way our words are being received, the notes being taken, the drift of ideas. But a lecture somehow, with considerable repressions, allows the illusion to be maintained. I will come back to the paradoxes of the lecture in a moment.

The tutorial is more threatening, and some teachers are plainly terrified of them – of immanent chaos? What is potentially disruptive to the communication model is the fact that students are expected to speak in tutorials. In order to maintain the illusion of presence of the teacher, students are required to speak in ways which reinforce their passivity. This is a speaking which is simultaneously a silencing, a not speaking. The tutorial paper presentation is the best example of this, an excruciating and boring experience for all concerned: the public display of testing of knowledge. There is something gratuitous about this ritual of humiliation since this is a speaking to which no one is listening, neither students *nor* teacher. It's boring because there is no space to speak. The tutorial paper is a representation of the lecture or the reading, and thus the student is likely to be interrupted and corrected on the adequacy of this representation. The tutor might also decide to jolt him- or herself out of boredom by cutting the paper short and presenting a lecture. Other students watch in stunned silence. Look at their watches. Write shopping lists. Dream of being not there.

These silencing strategies might be understood as attempts to refuse the possibility of the student becoming teacher, attempts to master the fear of a student proposing a different reading or asking a question to which one has no ready-made answer, thereby positioning the teacher as student. The notion of a singular reading – part and parcel of the communication model – further props up a monologic position of the teacher: 'Why do students need to say anything?' 'Why do we need tutorials?' is the logical extension.

A monologic speaking position on the part of the teacher is supported by the usual composition of classes, namely, one teacher and many students. Both teachers and students are often extraordinarily resistant to changes to this structure. Teachers tend to be threatened by notions of team teaching and peer-review, going so far sometimes as to invoke rights to privacy and confidentiality. And students almost automatically speak through and to the teacher in tutorials, rather than to each other. Does looking to the teacher for truth make the student's speech feel more secure? ('I'll be told if I've got it right or wrong and that's it.') In our teaching, in order to break with a singular position of truth, we look for ways of showing the relation between teachers, which include teaching in each other's presence and even speaking to each other in lectures. And in tutorials, one of my strategies for breaking the tendency for students to speak through the singular teacher is to encourage them to take up teacher–supervisor positions in relation to each other ('be the supervisor you would like to have').

If we let go of the fear of speech and the desire to control and instead welcome the unpredictable, it is possible to get a sense of ideas happening, here, now, in the classroom; of knowledge in process, rather than complete. When this is happening in tutorials I feel energised, by a dynamic over which I have no control, which is not to suggest that this is a speaking without an initial order set by the teacher. Barthes gives a sense of the 'high' that can come of allowing a multiplicity of voices:

> Where is speech? In locution? In listening? In the *returns* of the one and the other? The problem is not to abolish the distinction in functions (*teacher/student* – after all, as Sade has taught us, order is one of the guarantees of pleasure) but to protect the instability and, as it were, the giddying whirl of the positions of speech. (1977: 205–6)

This would be to keep desire alive – 'the *returns* of the one and the other' – and ensure a constant displacement for all in teaching. Should he ever find his place, Barthes goes on to say, he would give up teaching.

The displacing effects of speech are a consequence of these returns and also of the embodiment of speech: 'the voice is located at the articulation of body and discourse' (Barthes 1985: 255). I am nowhere more aware of this than when I am lecturing. I can feel my body speaking, the sheer physical effort alone, although it is more than this that makes the speech of the lecture embodied. Emotion. An affective living of ideas in the speaking. What repressions must go on to imagine that it is disembodied consciousness that gives a lecture, to maintain the illusions of presence, of the concept, of self-consciousness? Or to imagine that ideas are received as pure, clear ideas? For what is heard in teaching is the *voice*, with all the variations in quality, from the amplified voice of the lecture to the private, sometimes intimate voice of the tutorial. However much academics might disavow their bodies, the student audience of a lecture listens with eyes as well as ears, with emotion, with their bodies. (Think of the comments that students make in evaluations, the sorts of things they notice about our gestures, clothes, movements, things that often make us squirm and certainly unsettle any illusions about the sacredness of the teacher.)

Although the lecture might seem to be monologic, with an oppositional speaking–listening structure, I want to suggest not only that it can be dialogic, but also that it needs to be, if it is to work. It is very difficult lecturing to a passive audience; imagine lecturing to no audience at all. The performance of ideas needs an active listening. But what do I mean by working? For me, maybe it is that a lecture needs to reverberate. For a lecture to work it must reverberate in the audience, which is not to imply that it is received in the same way by everyone, nor that it reverberates for everyone. However, in a reverberation an image comes to life, it is experienced sensually, felt, rather than regarded abstractly. And the reverberation works on both sides, in both the reception and the performance: images–ideas need to reverberate in the lecturer as well as the audience.

Let me say a little about my experience of this. I understand that what I am doing is literally embodying ideas in performance. Thus I need to go through rituals of preparation, taking up the ideas that I will speak, so that by the time I'm in the lecture theatre they will feel part of me; they will speak me. Needing an audience, there is nevertheless a quite intense relation with oneself in this process of immersion in the speaking of ideas. We might understand 'thinking on one's feet' as a sort of internal dialogue that requires a third term, the other of the audience. The lecture's success in bringing ideas to life depends on an openness to the risks involved in this exchange. For this reason I never write out lecture notes, I never *write* a lecture, using instead messy and almost illegible notes. This is done quite deliberately, to help me speak.

This experience underscores the difference between the medium of writing and that of speech and the importance of speech to teaching. There is a difference between someone read-ing from a written piece, a paper or a lecture, and someone speaking. Speaking is a bodily performance. Reading from a writ-ing can deny this performative aspect. Speaking brings out the immediacy in the mediation of the lecture: an enactment of ideas in the physical presence of others, which is what makes it, if per-formed, such an engaging form. Referring to the difference between writing a book and lecturing, Bachelard says: 'When we are lecturing, we become animated by the joy of teaching and, at times, our words think for us' (1969: xxxv). That's it: the sensual pleasure of words thinking for us when we speak–teach.

* * *

> I listen to my relation with the body . . . singing . . . and that relation is erotic (Barthes 1977: 188)

Is it possible for a lecture to sing? I like this idea. Whether or not it is possible, and certainly Barthes makes a distinction between the performance-voice of music and the speech of teaching, there is a point of connection between these two forms: the erotic rela-tion between bodies. Teaching is not merely informative but an emotional embodied experience, constituted in desire. Thus, like writing, reading and singing, when the teaching relation lives, when it reverberates, it is erotic.

> It is hard to decide whether what affected us more . . . was our con-cern with the sciences that we were taught or with . . . our teachers. . . . In many of us *the path to the sciences led only through our teachers.* (Freud, quoted in Felman 1982: 34)

Falling in love with one's teachers is such a common story. Seduction and fantasies of seduction, of student by teacher, of teacher by student, are almost everyday in the world of teaching (Barthes 1977: 196-7). Love and knowledge are so intertwined in their powers of motivation. In *Managing* we said that writing for pleasure involves writing simultaneously for oneself and for an other. This is to write for the love of an other: whether or not we ever meet that other, the writing–reading relation is erotic. I have always written for my teachers, for the love of my teachers, and I now write also for the students who are my teachers.

Erotic relations between students and teachers take all sorts of forms. To wish such relations away, or, more frighteningly, as is happening in some universities, to outlaw such relations, won't make them disappear. This is to misunderstand and indeed deny the deep connection between the erotic and knowledge (Irigaray 1993: 20-33). It might be more productive to pose the issue in terms of different models of desire and a choice between them. For example, Freud, in the previous quotation, is referring to a love for the Father, for the one 'presumed to know'. We have spoken of this in terms of a prevailing familial model of desire in knowledge, a desire that is possessive and not open to otherness. For an alternative approach to erotic relations in teaching I would turn again to Barthes and Cixous.

Whenever Barthes makes reference to such relations, and he *does*, without romanticising, acknowledging the difficulties and the futilities in a realisation of desire (1977: 196–7), there is a sense of lightness in the erotic and pleasure in the process of mutual seduction and fantasy. I want to be seduced by students' work, engaged by their writing, just as I would seduce in lecturing: 'The text you write must prove to me *that it desires me*' (Barthes 1975: 6). And somehow, a student essay *can* seduce in a way that even Barthes or Cixous cannot, precisely because it comes out of the exchange of teaching. There is something about the dialogue, the to and fro of ideas coming alive, the *relation*, that produces a high. The skill is in keeping this ever so light.

Serious, even intense, but light: this is Cixous's vision of a graceful desiring relation: a combination of attachment and *detachment* (Cixous 1992: 68–73; Renshaw 1994). Cixous's understanding of intimate distance, detached intimacy, of moments that can't be held, might be compared with Baudelaire's fleeting, elusive love:

— O lovely fugitive,
I am suddenly reborn from your swift glance;
Shall I never see you till eternity?

Somewhere, far off! too late! *never*, perchance!
Neither knows where the other goes or lives;
We might have loved, and you knew this might be!
                    (as quoted in Benjamin 1973:45)

For me, Cixous's fleeting desire suggests a positive way of imagining the erotic in teaching. But of course her model of desire has broader implications for understandings of knowledge. As we will see in the next chapter, the combination of proximity and difference is crucial to a passionate way of thinking about the nature of our relation with our world.

Knowing

Sensual representations are in a perpetual flux; they come after each other like the waves of a river, and even during the time that they last, they do not remain the same thing. . . . We are never sure of again finding a perception such as we experienced it the first time; for if the thing perceived has not changed, it is we who are no longer the same. (Durkheim 1976: 433)

What a lovely description of duration, or irreversible time, the time of sensual lived experience. But this troubles Durkheim. It disturbs his understanding scientific knowledge.

Durkheim is distinguishing 'the concept' from sensual representations as a way of setting out what is involved in a scientific sociology. In the process, he clearly articulates assumptions which inform much sociology. But perhaps more significantly, he makes explicit the exclusions on which this knowledge depends: the flux of sensual representations, for example, which unsettle a scientific fixing or grasping of an object. It is as if Durkheim's eloquent insight into the way life is experienced must itself be transcended, by science. But still he can't help but acknowledge this experience, and in writing, retain something of the sensual quality of it. What we can find in Durkheim then is a tension between 'knowledge' understood as something that is held or possessed, and what I shall refer to as 'knowing', a knowledge *process* that does not attempt to transcend or master sensual experience, but, rather, is itself in duration.

Both the subject and the object of knowledge change in the flux of sensually experienced life. In Durkheim's view, science must attain a form of stability and certainty over and above this flux. Thus 'the concept' is 'opposed to sensual representations'; it is 'outside of time and change', 'it resists change'. 'It is a manner of thinking that, at every moment of time, is fixed and crystal-lized' – solid and stable, 'immutable', 'impersonal' (1976: 433–6). To this end science requires a suppression of the senses and sensual life; a suppression of particularity in rhythms of life, experiences of time; and a suppression of particularity in experiences of space. Science needs abstract notions of time and space for these allow generalisations and a conception of the whole. 'The category *par excellence* would seem to be this very concept of *totality*, an abstraction which includes all things' (1976: 440–2). To achieve this scientific goal it is quite clear that any qualitative differences in experiences must be excluded. A principle of sameness and a refusal of process is at work here.

And from what position is this knowing of the whole taking place? From 'outside and above'. The subject of knowledge remains outside and distinct from the object of knowledge in order that it might represent or *grasp* that object or, in other words, be objective. 'Being placed outside of and above individual and local contingencies . . . at every moment of time, it embraces all known reality' (Durkheim 1976: 444). It occupies a God-like position.

Durkheim's fantastic desire to know the whole has echoes in much contemporary sociology – in forms of writing that are abstracted and distanced from the object, and in the choice and constitution of objects. This is quite apparent in sociological categories such as society, capitalism, modernity, post-modernity, the family, the city and so on. But such a desire also, often quite explicitly, motivates sociological approaches to social change. A common sociological concern is to identify the source of change; either, quite grandly, *the* source of social change ('Have social movements replaced the working class?'), or the source of change in a specific field of research, such as health, welfare, education. Sociologists would be masters of social change, and, thus, the future: 'I will identify the source and end of change; I will master, orchestrate, control change.' And, thus, *deny* change. For to know and master change one must, with Durkheim, imagine oneself to be outside and above life, contingency, process.

Sociologists' attempts to flee sensual lived experience can be understood as expressions of Hegelian desire. It will be recalled that, for Hegel, knowledge is self-knowledge: a desire to know the whole is a desire to know the *self* as whole and coherent, to possess the truth of self-certainty. In Hegelian terms, this desire for self-presence entails a negative relation to otherness. Such a desire can also be found in the scientific exclusions that Durkheim includes in his text. Durkheim acknowledges that in sensual experience things change, but his desire is for a knowledge that would control and master the unstable. This can be understood as a desire for certainty and stability in the self; as a desire for presence – presence of the past as a present, presence of the object to the self, and *self-presence*. This is a desire which, as we can read in Durkheim and Hegel, ultimately fails.

For Durkheim's science to hold out the promise of stability and self-presence 'the concept' must repress transformation and the time of duration. But what is repressed does not go away. However much a knowledge might imagine itself free of or abstracted from experience in the sensual world, this is nevertheless an imagining. An abstracted knowledge is itself a particular sort of experience, even if it would deny it. What is so wonderful about Durkheim is that his whole thesis in the *Elementary Forms of Religious Life* is about the social basis of forms of knowledge that deny their sociality. In short, Durkheim can be read in a positive way against himself: his own understanding of the social nature of religion and knowledge undoes his account of science.

Durkheim's famous sacred/profane distinction has been crucial to our analyses of sociological knowledge practices. Douglas has used this distinction in an internal critical reading of Durkheim demonstrating that his theory of the sacred itself becomes sacred (1975: ix–xxi; see also Taussig 1992: 119–29). Durkheim's thesis is that although the sacred is produced as something standing outside and above the profane of everyday life, it is in fact a product of, a projection or idealisation of the social (1976: 422). Durkheim regarded his theory of religion as the basis of a sociology of knowledge. The irony, as Douglas points out, is that he made an exception of his own theory in the name of science. We can ask of Durkheim his own question: how can a knowledge be positioned outside and above, uncontaminated by the flux of life, the sensual, the particularity of experiences? What is sacred is contested; it is not immutable, fixed and given. Fortunately.

* * *

A deconstruction of the sacred/profane distinction demonstrates the ways in which the sacred depends upon and bears the traces of the profane. A deconstructive strategy is concerned with undoing the principle of oppositions by which one term would presume to stand unto itself, as a presence, through a denial of another term. An oppositional principle informs Durkheim's conception of knowledge; my concern has been to undo this, or to put his texts to work in an internal undoing. Let me be more specific about this strategy.

First, I want to reiterate that this is a positive strategy; a deconstruction is not a debunking exercise. My concern is not to show that Durkheim got it wrong, that he thought he'd defined science, but failed. Rather, the contention here, and indeed throughout this book, is that a recognition that scientific fantasy is impossible opens up all sorts of creative possibilities for knowledge and science.

The oppositions to which I particularly want to draw attention are those between abstraction and sensual experience, and stasis and movement, as found in Durkheim's account of knowledge. I am interested in a form of knowledge that positively values the subordinate term, a knowledge practice that participates in the fluidity of sensual experience. To privilege the subordinate term does not amount to a simple reversal, to a negation of any notion of stable knowledge or to a refusal of abstractions. If we simply reverse the terms, nothing of the oppositional structure changes; the desire for mastery remains, a desire that one term stand alone to the exclusion of others. But the privileging of the subordinate term through a reversal does *allow for* the possibility of a displacement of this structure. For the negated and repressed term embodies a different principle of meaning, one that is disruptive to a fixing of terms as discrete static oppositional identities. In this book we have described this principle of movement as 'the relational', the movement of relations between terms.

What are the implications of this principle for ways of knowing? It suggests that we might think of a knowledge process involving a movement back and forth between lived sensual experience and more abstracted forms of thought, and that indeed abstractions themselves might be experienced sensually, *lived*. I would be the last to deny the attraction of abstractions. Look at this discussion – it has been abstract. I can feel quite passionate about abstractions, and take a great pleasure in them just as I imagine some mathematicians do. The important point is that I would make no claims about an abstracted knowledge being closer to the truth: there are just different forms of knowledge. I am also aware of taking refuge in abstractions at times: when discussions of teaching relations have become too close to home, when I feel uncertain about the messiness of the day to day experience of teaching, I have shifted to a more abstract level, quoting Cixous, for a cooler distance.

Another way of putting this would be in terms of a movement between intellectual and intuitive forms of thinking, or a movement between distance and proximity. I am aware of this movement in the process of writing this book: the book proposal is rather abstract (although based on gut-feelings or intuitions) and I feel unsure of the implications of what is set out in it; I write intuitively to that proposal, not quite knowing what I am doing, but feeling immersed, very close to the writing–ideas; I then stand back and, from something of a distance, do a close reading of my writing – an intellectual moment. Both moments, intuitive and intellectual, it seems to me, can be *lived*, albeit in different ways.

If we approach this issue in terms of the stasis–movement distinction, the implication is not that we simply value movement, but that knowledge be imagined as a process of moments, brief moments, of stasis within movement: a having without holding (Cixous 1992: 56–9, 67–8; Irigaray 1993: 14). So to return to the distinction with which I framed this chapter: *knowing* might be thought of as an ongoing process of engagement with our world which undoes knowledge as something that is held, complete and coherent. But it also seems important to me that we acknowledge that we do *have* knowledge – that it is not all undifferentiated flow and process; there are resting points, moments when we say 'that's it'. The issue is how, without grasping, might we have these, and also move on.

It is possible that the experience of 'that's it', the experience of an idea coming alive for us, ringing true, allows for precisely this – a having in movement. When ideas come alive, we are moved by them. This is also a moment when the abstract and the sensual come together.

* * *

I now want to turn to phenomenology, a philosophical tradition which quite explicitly values the experience that is excluded in scientific sociological discourse. Acknowledging sensual and emotional dimensions of knowledge processes, phenomenology has contributed greatly to this book's accounts of passionate ways of *knowing*. Elsewhere I have referred to Bachelard; here I will focus mainly on Merleau-Ponty, another major figure in this tradition.

The two central ideas in phenomenology are 'experience' and 'the phenomenon'. The phenomenological project is one of getting at the specific quality of any phenomenon via experience, Merleau-Ponty seeking a philosophy which 'offers an account of space, time and the world as we "live" them' (1962: vii). This concern with a knowledge that addresses the specificity of phenomena and the particularity of lived experience contrasts with Durkheim's account of science; here we have the positive valuation of that which Durkheim suppressed. If phenomenological knowing is experiencing, then it is *in* the world, not, as Durkheim would have it, presuming to stand outside:

> since we are in the world, since indeed our reflections are carried out in the temporal flux onto which we are trying to seize . . . there is no thought which embraces all our thought. (Merleau-Ponty 1962: xiv; see also 1964: 109)

This inability to stand outside the world we study is not a problem for Merleau-Ponty; indeed how could we know the world if we were not of it? As this philosophical tradition sees it, what is problematic is the notion of a distinction between subject and object, the assumption that the world is a space 'given to begin with', external to the subject (see Bergson 1991: 231; Merleau-Ponty 1962: 154; 1968: 130). The very formulation 'experiencing the phenomenon' disrupts a distinction between subject and object of knowledge, pointing instead to a *relation between*.

Knowing, then, takes place in an encounter between self and the world, with no attempt to transcend or master the sensual world or the encounter with it. Knowing is in life. Thus it is an experience that is thoroughly embodied and affective. We know the world, or specific phenomena, through our affective, emotional, sensual responses: 'this is how I feel in the face of . . .'. This is to be understood as an active rather than a passive perception. Merleau-Ponty speaks of 'taking up' or 'living' a situation (1962: 157). And in this process things change.

Change crucially distinguishes *knowing* from a knowledge that is possessed. Recall that for Durkheim science is a 'manner of thinking that, at every moment of time, is fixed and crystallized' (1976: 433). To possess, to grasp, is to fix. Denial of change in either the subject or object of knowledge necessitates a denial of a relation between, for as soon as we think of the subject and object in connection it becomes difficult to imagine things staying unchanged. The assimilation implied by grasping admits of no relation; this is simply the other side to distance and opposition. The idea of experience, on the other hand, focuses attention on the relation as constitutive. Because the self and the phenomenon affect each other in the encounter there can be no ultimate possession or end of knowledge (see, e.g., Irigaray 1993: 185).

Questions about the relation between subject and object of knowledge are questions of desire: the relation between the self and the world is a self–other relation. A knowledge practice which privileges experience parallels Cixousian desire in its acknowledgement of the *relation* or movement between terms. For Merleau-Ponty and Cixous, the process of knowing requires a combination of proximity and distance in the relation between the self and the phenomenon, the other. The closeness requires a difference, or a certain distance implied by difference (see also Simmel 1994), for without difference there would simply be one, an identity. This is important because proximity and connection are sometimes taken to imply a merging and thus lack of difference. Merleau-Ponty questioned Bergson's privileging of intuition to the exclusion of the intellect on precisely these grounds, arguing that Bergson's desire for intuitive immediacy erased any difference or relation between self and the world (1962: 57). By closing the gap completely in a return to the immediate, Bergson's intuition denies process and the relational just as much as an abstracted intellectual approach to the world does in its desire for coincidence through distance and separation.

In contemporary discussions, this issue arises in connection with a valorisation of metaphors of touch in the work of people such as Irigaray and Merleau-Ponty. For Irigaray touch disrupts identity, implying a relation of difference between terms that are

contiguous, whereas metaphors of sight invite notions of coincidence (1985: 25-9). In his later work, Merleau-Ponty's interest in
touch is associated with the elusive notion of flesh, through
which he also refigures vision:

> What there is then are not things first identical with themselves,
> which would then offer themselves to the seer, nor is there a seer who
> is first empty and who, afterward, would open himself to them –
> but something to which we could not be closer than by palpating it
> with our look, things we could not dream of seeing 'all naked'
> because the gaze itself envelops them, clothes them with its own
> flesh. (1968: 131)

It is striking that Merleau-Ponty's metaphors for vision are
those of touch: 'palpate', 'envelop'. Not only is he questioning the
common association of sight with distance, but he is also saying
that the senses are not separate, distinct, at a distance: they 'sub-
tend and overlap each other'. The principle of proximity and
difference is thus applied to the relation between the senses
(Merleau-Ponty 1968: 133; see also Irigaray 1993: 151–84).

Flesh is the concept that captures this principle. Merleau-Ponty
understands this as an elemental form which simultaneously connects and differentiates subjects and 'things' of the world. 'The
flesh' is what bodies have in common and it is that which marks
out their specificity. Embodying a principle of same and different,
it is the in-between. He speaks of an 'intimacy' between the visible and us, 'as close as between the sea and the strand' (1968:
130–1). A relation of intimacy means that it is difficult to tell
where one begins and the other ends, to draw distinctions; a
boundary is crossed, yet qualitative difference and specificity
remain.

'The flesh' and metaphors of touch suggest that we are in the
midst of the world we would know. But more than this, they
suggest a *sensual* relation with our world – that knowing might
be a sensual experience (and this comes across in the way
Irigaray and Merleau-Ponty write about this relation). Such an
experience unsettles any conception of a 'subject that already
knows its objects and controls its relations with the world and
with others' (Irigaray 1993: 185). 'Sensual pleasure', Irigaray
says, 'can return to the evanescence of subject and object' (1993:

185). The sensual – so feared by Durkheim – is welcomed by a knowledge that has no desire to pin down or control, a knowledge that would remain open to change and the unforeseeable.

* * *

I suspect that this sounds rather abstract, so let me suggest how a phenomenological analysis might proceed. I want to take the example of travel, choosing it because quests, exploration and discovery are commonplace motifs for knowledge (Van Den Abbeele 1992: xiii–xxx). The metaphoric transfer works both ways: in speaking of experiences of travel, I also speak of ways of knowing, of forms of relation between self and the world, self and the other.

So, in connection with travel, a phenomenologist might consider the *experience* in terms of the form of movement, the structure of the journey, the technology of travel, the mediations involved. We cannot assume the nature of relations between the self and the world, for these are constituted by particular forms of mediation. As Simmel so brilliantly observes, for example, both the door and the bridge connect and separate, but in different ways (1994). If we were thinking of train travel we might ask: What are the implications of glass, moving glass, for how we experience the relation with the world 'outside' the window? The implications of the railway lines? The form of rhythm of the train? How does this transport technology affect our perceptions of time–space? What senses are involved? How does this affect our perception of space, our relation with our world? What is our experience, in terms of time and space, of the relation between points of departure and arrival in the railway journey, and the in-between space (Schivelbusch 1979)? And what about the emotions associated with this, with 'arrival', with 'departure', with being 'in-between'? (And here, might I not be asking questions about reading or writing a text, or listening to a story or delivering a lecture?)

Such questions unavoidably raise comparisons: to specify the experience of train travel I must consider other forms of movement and technologies of transport – planes, cars and walking for example – and different sorts of journey. In doing so I move between details of experience and complex, abstract ideas.

Difficult questions around forms of temporality and spatiality, for example, are being addressed through specific analyses of everyday experiences.

By asking questions about the relation between the self and the world, a phenomenological account of train travel would be implicitly an analysis of a way of knowing. As we have emphasised throughout this book, forms of knowledge can be distinguished in terms of the mediations involved: the mediations of train travel invite different ways of knowing from those of walking, and different again from those of plane travel. There is a difference between a lecture and a tutorial, and between a sociology textbook and Bachelard. Some forms of media invite fantasies of a mediation-free direct knowledge or a knowledge based on distance and coincidence, an abstracted knowledge. But these are mediated and experiential knowledges, even if they would deny it.

* * *

I could take any example from everyday life and look at the forms of knowledge involved, but travel is particularly suggestive because of movement. It is not surprising to find a metaphoric play with travel, journeys and knowledge running through the writings of someone like Cixous. Her desire in knowledge is for a movement towards the other, without any desire for appropriation of the other, or for an end. Any return would be a return with difference. This is a knowledge that delights in its journey, a knowledge that takes pleasure in the strange.

Without denigrating the many pleasures of travel, I want to end with the joy of the first encounter: the wonder in the face of the new. Wonder is a value in knowledge that has inspired this book. There would be no point to knowledge, I think, if we did not feel a passion for wonder, seeing the same as different, the familiar as strange. I associate this passion for knowledge with what Nietzsche refers to as the will to life, 'the eternal joy of becoming' (1976: 562–3). In her reading of Descartes, Irigaray says that we need to have wonder to move *towards*. Wonder is the passion that allows us to be 'faithful to the perpetual newness of the self, the other, the world' (1993: 73–6, 82).

Merleau-Ponty speaks of 'wonder in the face of the world',

saying that a phenomenologist is 'a perpetual beginner', seeing things always as if for the first time (1962: xiii–xiv). To acknowledge the permanent child in us, which this certainly implies, is not to indulge in a fantasy of innocent knowledge. Rather it would be to say: 'I know that I know, but I would forget knowing in order to be open to the new.' Bachelard says just this in his account of the poetic nature of phenomenological knowledge. 'Non-knowing is not a form of ignorance but a difficult transcendence of knowledge. . . . In poetry, non-knowing is a primal condition' (1969: xxviii–xxix). Bachelard constantly says that a poetic–phenomenological image could never work in terms of re-presentation of a past image, a holding on. An image must be lived by a poetic subject, and to be lived it must be relived as if new, as if for the first time. It must come alive.

Wonder, I am suggesting, has religious overtones – we feel awe and inspiration in the face of the other, otherness. It involves a faith in the new. But this is a religious experience that is not about a withdrawal from life: wonder is a religious experience in *life*, in the world. It involves an encounter, an engagement with the sensual world.

References

Abraham, J.H. (ed.) (1973) *The Origins and Growth of Sociology*. Ringwood: Penguin.

Aristotle (1941) *Basic Works of Aristotle*. Ed. R. McKeon. New York: Random House.

Aristotle (1987) *A New Aristotle Reader*. Ed. J.L. Ackrill. Oxford: Clarendon.

Aristotle (1991) *The Art of Rhetoric*. Tr. H.C. Lawson-Tancred. Ringwood: Penguin.

Aron, R. (1965) *Main Currents in Sociological Thought, 1 and 2*. Ringwood: Penguin.

Atkins, G.D. (1992) *Estranging the Familiar: Toward a Revitalized Critical Writing*. Athens, GA: University of Georgia Press.

Atkinson, P. (1990) *The Ethnographic Imagination*. London: Routledge.

Auden, W.H. (1976) *Collected Poems*. Ed. E. Mendelson. London: Faber & Faber.

Auerbach, E. (1968) *Mimesis*. Tr. W.R. Trask. Princeton: Princeton University Press.

Bachelard, G. (1969) *The Poetics of Space*. Tr. M. Jolas. Boston: Beacon Press.

Bachelard, G. (1971) *The Poetics of Reverie*. Tr. D. Russell. Boston: Beacon Press.

Bachelard, G. (1983) *Water and Dreams: An Essay on the Imagination of Matter*. Tr. E. Farrell. Dallas: Pegasus.

Barthes, R. (1973) *Mythologies*. Tr. A. Lavers. London: Paladin.

Barthes, R. (1975) *The Pleasure of the Text*. Tr. R. Miller. New York: Hill & Wang.

Barthes, R. (1977) *Image–Music–Text*. Tr. S. Heath. Glasgow: Collins-Fontana.

Barthes, R. (1985) *The Responsibility of Forms*. Tr. R. Howard. New York: Hill & Wang.

Barthes, R. (1986) *The Rustle of Language*. Tr R. Howard. Oxford: Basil Blackwell.

Barthes, R. (1991) *The Grain of the Voice*. Tr. L. Coverdale. Berkeley: University of California Press.

Barthes, R. (1992) *Incidents*. Tr. R. Howard. Berkeley and Los Angeles: University of California Press.

Bemelmans, L. (1992) *Madeline*. London: Scholastic.

Benjamin, W. (1970) *Illuminations*. Tr. H. Zohn. London: Fontana.

Benjamin, W. (1973) *Charles Baudelaire: A Lyric Poetic in the Era of High Capitalism*. Tr. H. Zohn. London: New Left Books.

Benjamin, W. (1978) *Reflections*. Tr. E. Jephcott. New York: Schocken.

Berger, J. (1984) *And Our Faces, My Heart, Brief as Photos*. London: Writers and Readers.

Berger, J. (1985) *Pig Earth*. London: Chatto & Windus.

Berger, J. (1989) *Once in Europa*. Cambridge: Granta.

Berger, J. (1991) *Lilac and Flag*. Cambridge: Granta.

Bergson, H. (1991) *Matter and Memory*. Tr. N.M. Paul and W.S. Palmer. New York: Zone Books.

Borges, J.L. (1970) *Labyrinths*. Ringwood: Penguin.

Brown, N.O. (1966) *Love's Body*. New York: Vintage Books.

Bruner, J. (1990) *Acts of Meaning*. Cambridge, MA: Harvard University Press.

Burke, K. (1961) *The Rhetoric of Religion*. Boston: Beacon Press.

Butor, M. (1992) 'Travel and Writing', in M. Kowalewski (ed.), *Temperamental Journeys*. Athens, GA: University of Georgia Press.

Calvino, I. (1982) *If on a Winter's Night a Traveler*. London: Picador.

Calvino, I. (1989) *The Literature Machine*. London: Picador.

Calvino, I. (1993) *The Road to San Giovanni*. London: Jonathan Cape.

Carter, P. (1988) *The Road to Botany Bay*. London: Faber & Faber.

de Certeau, M. (1984) *The Practice of Everyday Life*. Tr. S.F. Rendall. Berkeley and Los Angeles: University of California Press.

Chatwin, B. (1988) *The Songlines*. London: Picador.

Chukovsky, N. (1963) *From Two to Five*. Tr. M. Morton. Berkeley: University of California Press.

Cixous, H. (1986) 'Sorties: Out and Out: Attacks/Ways Out/Forays', in H. Cixous and C. Clément, *The Newly Born Woman*. Tr. B. Wing. Manchester: Manchester University Press.

Cixous, H. (1988) *Writing Differences: Readings from the Seminar of Hélène Cixous*. Ed. S. Sellers. Milton Keynes: Open University Press.

Cixous, H. (1992) *Readings: The Poetics of Blanchot, Joyce, Kafka, Kleist, Lispector and Tsvetayeva*. Tr. V. Conley. New York: Harvester Wheatsheaf.

Cixous, H. (1993) *Three Steps on the Ladder of Writing*. Tr. S. Cornell and S. Sellers. New York: Columbia University Press.

Clifford, J. and Marcus, G. (1986) *Writing Culture*. Berkeley: University of California Press.

Comte, A. (1973) 'Extracts from *The Positive Philosophy*', in J.H. Abraham (ed.), *The Origins and Growth of Sociology*. Ringwood: Penguin.

Coser, L. (1971) *Masters of Sociological Thought*. New York: Harcourt Brace Jovanovich.

Crites, S. (1989) 'The Narrative Quality of Experience', in S. Hauerwas and L.G. Jones (eds), *Why Narrative?* Grand Rapids, MI: William B. Eerdmans.

Daniel, A. (1983) *Power, Privilege and Prestige*. Melbourne: Longman Cheshire.

Deleuze, G. and Guattari, F. (1994) *What is Philosophy?* Tr. G. Burchell and H. Tomlinson. London: Verso.

Derrida, J. (1978) *Writing and Difference*. Tr. A. Bass. Chicago: University of Chicago Press.

Derrida, J. (1987) *Positions*. Tr. A. Bass. London: Athlone Press.

Douglas, M. (1970) *Purity and Danger*. Harmondsworth: Penguin.

Douglas, M. (1975) *Implicit Meanings*. London: Routledge & Kegan Paul.

Durkheim, E. (1964) *The Rules of Sociological Method*. Tr. S.A. Solovay and J.H. Mueller. New York: Free Press.

Durkheim, E. (1976) *The Elementary Forms of the Religious Life*. Tr. J.W. Swain. London: George Allen & Unwin.

Eco, U. (1992) *Interpretation and Overinterpretation*. Ed. S. Collini. Cambridge: Cambridge University Press.

Eco, U. (1994) *Six Walks in the Fictional Woods*. Cambridge, MA and London: Harvard University Press.

Eliade, M. (1954) *The Myth of the Eternal Return*. New York: Pantheon.

Elias, N. (1982) *The History of Manners*. Tr. E. Jephcott. New York: Pantheon.

Felman, S. (1982) 'Psychoanalysis and Education: Teaching Terminable and Interminable', in B. Johnson (ed.), *The Pedagogical Imperative: Teaching as a Literary Genre*. *Yale French Studies*, 63: 21–44.

Fingarette, H. (1972) *Confucius*. New York: Harper & Row.

Forster, E.M. (1962) *Aspects of the Novel*. Harmondsworth: Penguin.

Foucault, M. (1977a) *Discipline and Punish*. Tr. A. Sheridan. Ringwood: Penguin.

Foucault, M. (1977b) *Language, Counter-Memory, Practice*. Tr. D.F. Bouchard and S. Simon. Ithaca: Cornell University Press.

Foucault, M. (1981) *The History of Sexuality*. Tr. R. Hurley. Ringwood: Penguin.

Foucault, M. (1982) 'The Subject and Power', in H.L. Dreyfus and P. Rabinow, *Michel Foucault*. Chicago: University of Chicago Press.

Foucault, M. (1984) *The Foucault Reader*. Ed. P. Rabinow. New York: Pantheon.

Frazer, J. (1993) *The Golden Bough*. Ware: Wordsworth.

Freud, S. (1960) *Totem and Taboo*. Tr. J. Strachey. London: Routledge & Kegan Paul.

Freud, S. (1973) *New Introductory Lectures of Psycho-Analysis*. Tr. J. Strachey. Ringwood: Penguin.

Freud, S. (1986) 'On Narcissism', in A.P. Morrison (ed.), *Essential Papers on Narcissism*. New York: New York University Press.

Gallop, J. (1994) 'The Teacher's Breasts', in J.J. Matthews (ed.), *Jane Gallop Seminar Papers*. Canberra: Humanities Research Centre, The Australian National University.

Giddens, A. (1989) *Sociology*. Cambridge: Polity Press.

Goffman, E. (1972) *Relations in Public*. Ringwood: Penguin.

Hegel, G.W.F. (1977) *Phenomenology of Spirit*. Tr. A.V. Miller. Oxford: Oxford University Press.

Irigaray, L. (1985) *This Sex Which Is Not One*. Tr. C. Porter and C. Burke. New York: Cornell University Press.

Irigaray, L. (1993) *An Ethics of Sexual Difference*. Tr. C. Burke and G.C. Gill. London: Athlone Press.

Le Guin, U. (1989) *Dancing at the Edge of the World*. New York: Harper & Row.

Lévi-Strauss, C. (1966) *The Savage Mind*. Chicago: University of Chicago Press.

Lévi-Strauss, C. (1976) *Tristes Tropiques*. Tr. J. and D. Weightman. Harmondsworth: Penguin.

Lévi-Strauss, C. (1978) *Myth and Meaning*. London: Routledge.

Lévi-Strauss, C. (1986) *The Raw and the Cooked*. Tr. J. and D. Weightman. Ringwood: Penguin.

Lewis, I. (1976) *Social Anthropology in Perspective*. Ringwood: Penguin.

Maerth, O.K. (1974) *The Beginning Was the End*. London: Sphere.

Malouf, D. (1993) *Remembering Babylon*. Milsons Point: Random House.

Mandelstam, N. (1974) *Hope Abandoned*. Tr. M. Hayward. London: Collins & Harvill.

Marx, K. and Engels, F. (1971) *Manifesto of the Communist Party*. Moscow: Progress.

Merleau-Ponty, M. (1962) *Phenomenology of Perception*. Tr. C. Smith. London: Routledge & Kegan Paul.

Merleau-Ponty, M. (1964) *Signs*. Tr. R. McCleary. Evanston, IL: Northwestern University Press.

Merleau-Ponty, M. (1968) *The Visible and the Invisible*. Tr. A. Lingis. Evanston, IL: Northwestern University Press.

Mulkay, M.J. (1985) *The Word and the World*. London: George Allen & Unwin.

Murphy, R.F. (1981) 'Julian Steward', in S. Silverman (ed.), *Totems and Teachers*. New York: Columbia University Press.

Nadeau, M. (1973) *The History of Surrealism*. Tr. R. Howard. Ringwood: Penguin.

Nietzsche, F. (1976) *The Portable Nietzsche*. Ed. W. Kaufman. New York: Viking.

Pateman, C. (1988) *The Sexual Contract*. Cambridge: Polity Press.

Porter, D. (1994) 'Parody and Poetry', *Arena Magazine*, 14: 52–3.

Raison, T. (ed.) (1979) *The Founding Fathers of Social Science*. Rev. edn. P. Parker. London: Scolar Press.

Rapoport, J.L. (1991) *The Boy Who Couldn't Stop Washing*. New York: Signet.

Renshaw, S. (1994) *Desiring Death: A Movement Towards Grace*. Honours Thesis in Sociology, University of New South Wales.

Ricoeur, P. (1986) *The Rule of Metaphor*. Tr. R. Czerny. London: Routledge & Kegan Paul.

Sacks, O. (1986) *The Man Who Mistook His Wife For A Hat*. London: Picador.

Said, E.W. (1978) *Beginnings*. Baltimore: Johns Hopkins University Press.

Schivelbusch, W. (1979) *The Railroad Journey*. Tr. A. Hollo. New York: Urizen Books.

Sendak, M. (1977) 'The Artist as Author', in M. Meek, A. Warlow and G. Barton (eds), *The Cool Web*. London: Bodley Head.

Silverman, S. (ed.) (1981) *Totems and Teachers*. New York: Columbia University Press.

Simmel, G. (1950) *The Sociology of Georg Simmel*. Ed. and tr. K. Wolff. New York: Free Press.

Simmel, G. (1994) 'Bridge and Door', *Theory, Culture & Society*. 11 (1): 5–10.

Steiner, G. (1989) *Real Presences*. London: Faber & Faber.

Taussig, M. (1989) 'History as Commodity', *Critique of Anthropology*, 9 (1): 7–23.

Taussig, M. (1992) *The Nervous System*. New York: Routledge.

Taussig, M. (1993) *Mimesis and Alterity*. New York: Routledge.

Turner, V. (1969) *The Ritual Process*. Ringwood: Penguin.

Turner, V. (1970) *The Forest of Symbols*. Ithaca: Cornell University Press.

Turner, T. (1991) '"We are Parrots", "Twins are Birds"', in J.W. Fernandez (ed.), *Beyond Metaphor*. Stanford: Stanford University Press.

Van Den Abbeele, G. (1992) *Travel as Metaphor*. Minneapolis: University of Minnesota Press.

White, H. (1987) *The Content of the Form*. Baltimore: Johns Hopkins University Press.

Williams, R. (1971) *Orwell*. London: Fontana.

Worsley, P. (1984) *The Three Worlds*. London: Weidenfeld & Nicolson.

Index